Freedom of Information

Freedom of Information

Phill Jones

SERIES EDITOR
Alan Marzilli, M.A., J.D.

CHELSEA HOUSE
An Infobase Learning Company

Freedom of Information

Chelsea House
An imprint of Infobase Learning
132 West 31st Street
New York, NY 10001

Library of Congress Cataloging-in-Publication Data
Jones, Phill, 1953–
  Freedom of information / by Phill Jones.
  p. cm.—(Point/counterpoint)
  Includes bibliographical references and index.
  ISBN 978-1-60413-906-8 (hardcover)
  1. Freedom of information—United States—Juvenile literature. I. Title.
  KF5753.J66 2011
  342.7308'53—dc22
                              2011001008

Chelsea House books are available at special discounts when purchased in bulk quantities for businesses, associations, institutions, or sales promotions. Please call our Special Sales Department in New York at (212) 967-8800 or (800) 322-8755.

You can find Chelsea House on the World Wide Web at
http://www.infobaselearning.com.

Text design by Keith Trego
Cover design by Alicia Post
Composition by EJB Publishing Services
Cover printed by Yurchak Printing, Landisville, Pa.
Book printed and bound by Yurchak Printing, Landisville, Pa.

Printed in the United States of America

This book is printed on acid-free paper.

All links and Web addresses were checked and verified to be correct at the time of publication. Because of the dynamic nature of the Web, some addresses and links may have changed since publication and may no longer be valid.

B+T SP14. Recommended by C. Librarian from Richmond List.

Alan Marzilli, M.A., J.D.
Washington, D.C.

The POINT/COUNTERPOINT series offers the reader a greater understanding of some of the most controversial issues in contemporary
American society—issues such as capital punishment, immigration,
gay rights, and gun control. We have looked for the most contemporary issues and have included topics—such as the controversies
surrounding "blogging"—that we could not have imagined when the
series began.

In each volume, the author has selected an issue of particular
importance and set out some of the key arguments on both sides of the
issue. Why study both sides of the debate? Maybe you have yet to make
up your mind on an issue, and the arguments presented in the book
will help you to form an opinion. More likely, however, you will already
have an opinion on many of the issues covered by the series. There is
always the chance that you will change your opinion after reading the
arguments for the other side. But even if you are firmly committed to
an issue—for example, school prayer or animal rights—reading both
sides of the argument will help you to become a more effective advocate for your cause. By gaining an understanding of opposing arguments, you can develop answers to those arguments.

Perhaps more importantly, listening to the other side sometimes
helps you see your opponent's arguments in a more human way. For
example, Sister Helen Prejean, one of the nation's most visible oppo-
nents of capital punishment, has been deeply affected by her interactions with the families of murder victims. By seeing the families' grief
and pain, she understands much better why people support the death
penalty, and she is able to carry out her advocacy with a greater sensi-
tivity to the needs and beliefs of death penalty supporters.

The books in the series include numerous features that help the
reader to gain a greater understanding of the issues. Real-life examples
illustrate the human side of the issues. Each chapter also includes
excerpts from relevant laws, court cases, and other material, which
provide a better foundation for understanding the arguments. The

volumes contain citations to relevant sources of law and information, and an appendix guides the reader through the basics of legal research, both on the Internet and in the library. Today, through free Web sites, it is easy to access legal documents, and these books might give you ideas for your own research.

Studying the issues covered by the POINT/COUNTERPOINT series is more than an academic activity. The issues described in the books affect all of us as citizens. They are the issues that today's leaders debate and tomorrow's leaders will decide. While all of the issues covered in the POINT/COUNTERPOINT series are controversial today, and will remain so for the foreseeable future, it is entirely possible that the reader might one day play a central role in resolving the debate. Today it might seem that some debates—such as capital punishment and abortion—will never be resolved.

However, our nation's history is full of debates that seemed as though they never would be resolved, and many of the issues are now well settled—at least on the surface. In the nineteenth century, abolitionists met with widespread resistance to their efforts to end slavery. Ultimately, the controversy threatened the union, leading to the Civil War between the northern and southern states. Today, while a public debate over the merits of slavery would be unthinkable, racism persists in many aspects of society.

Similarly, today nobody questions women's right to vote. Yet at the beginning of the twentieth century, suffragists fought public battles for women's voting rights, and it was not until the passage of the Nineteenth Amendment in 1920 that the legal right of women to vote was established nationwide.

What makes an issue controversial? Often, controversies arise when most people agree that there is a problem but disagree about the best way to solve it. There is little argument that poverty is a major problem in the United States, especially in inner cities and rural areas. Yet, people disagree vehemently about the best way to address the problem. To some, the answer is social programs, such as welfare, food stamps, and public housing. However, many argue that such subsidies encourage dependence on government benefits while unfairly penalizing those who work and pay taxes, and that the real solution is to require people to support themselves.

American society is in a constant state of change, and sometimes modern practices clash with what many consider to be "traditional values," which are often rooted in conservative political views or religious beliefs. Many blame high crime rates, and problems such as poverty, illiteracy, and drug use on the breakdown of the traditional family structure of a married mother and father raising their children. Since the "sexual revolution" of the 1960s and 1970s, sparked in part by the widespread availability of the birth control pill, marriage rates have declined, and the number of children born outside of marriage has increased. The sexual revolution led to controversies over birth control, sex education, and other issues, most prominently abortion. Similarly, the gay rights movement has been challenged as a threat to traditional values. While many gay men and lesbians want to have the same right to marry and raise families as heterosexuals, many politicians and others have challenged gay marriage and adoption as a threat to American society.

Sometimes, new technology raises issues that we have never faced before, and society disagrees about the best solution. Are people free to swap music online, or does this violate the copyright laws that protect songwriters and musicians' ownership of the music that they create? Should scientists use "genetic engineering" to create new crops that are resistant to disease and pests and produce more food, or is it too risky to use a laboratory to create plants that nature never intended? Modern medicine has continued to increase the average lifespan—which is now 77 years, up from under 50 years at the beginning of the twentieth century—but many people are now choosing to die in comfort rather than living with painful ailments in their later years. For doctors, this presents an ethical dilemma: should they allow their patients to die? Should they assist patients in ending their own lives painlessly?

Perhaps the most controversial issues are those that implicate a Constitutional right. The Bill of Rights—the first 10 Amendments to the U.S. Constitution—spells out some of the most fundamental rights that distinguish our democracy from other nations with fewer freedoms. However, the sparsely worded document is open to interpretation, with each side saying that the Constitution is on their side. The Bill of Rights was meant to protect individual liberties; however, the needs of some individuals clash with society's needs. Thus, the Constitution often serves as a battleground between individuals and government officials seeking to protect society in some way. The First Amendment's guarantee of "freedom of speech" leads to some very difficult questions. Some forms of expression—such as burning an American flag—lead to public outrage, but are protected by the First Amendment. Other types of expression that most people find objectionable—such as child pornography—are not protected by the Constitution. The question is not only where to draw the line, but whether drawing lines around constitutional rights threatens our liberty.

The Bill of Rights raises many other questions about individual rights and societal "good." Is a prayer before a high school football game an "establishment of religion" prohibited by the First Amendment? Does the Second Amendment's promise of "the right to bear arms" include concealed handguns? Does stopping and frisking someone standing on a known drug corner constitute "unreasonable search and seizure" in violation of the Fourth Amendment? Although the U.S. Supreme Court has the ultimate authority in interpreting the U.S. Constitution, its answers do not always satisfy the public. When a group of nine people—sometimes by a five-to-four vote—makes a decision that affects hundreds of millions of others, public outcry can be expected. For example, the Supreme Court's 1973 ruling in *Roe v. Wade* that abortion is protected by the Constitution did little to quell the debate over abortion.

Whatever the root of the controversy, the books in the POINT/ COUNTERPOINT series seek to explain to the reader the origins of the debate, the current state of the law, and the arguments on either side of the debate. Our hope in creating this series is that readers will be better informed about the issues facing not only our politicians, but all of our nation's citizens, and become more actively involved in resolving these debates, as voters, concerned citizens, journalists, or maybe even elected officials.

This volume provides insight into the timely issues of government transparency and individual privacy. Although a number of earlier volumes in the POINT/COUNTERPOINT series have touched on these issues, laws and policies have developed rapidly in recent years. When we first examined these matters, the term "transparency" was used primarily in academic circles, but since the terrorist attacks of September 11, 2001, and the financial meltdown that began in late 2007, government transparency has become a key issue in each election cycle. Other high-profile events, such as the 2010 oil spill in the Gulf of Mexico and the failure of many "subprime" mortgages, have led activists to call for more information about industry practices. The effectiveness of the government's response to Hurricane Katrina in 2005 gave momentum to calls for more information about government disaster planning and agency operations. Because much information that is held by the government concerns military activities, private industry, and individual citizens, disclosure of such information often raises concerns regarding security and privacy. The delicate balance among these overlapping concerns is examined herein.

The Necessary, but Controversial, Right

I n November 2009, a reporter for the *New York Times* described a visit to a jail that the Central Intelligence Agency (CIA) had set up as part of the fight against terrorists:

> F.B.I. agents who arrived at a secret C.I.A. jail overseas in September 2002 found prisoners "manacled to the ceiling and subjected to blaring music around the clock," and a C.I.A. official wrote a list of questions for interrogators including "How close is each technique to the 'rack and screw,'" according to hundreds of pages of partly declassified documents released Friday by the Justice Department.[1]

The documents also revealed that U.S. Justice Department officials considered prosecuting one of the CIA interrogators.

How did the controversial actions of CIA agents and conflicts between government agencies become public knowledge? The American Civil Liberties Union (ACLU) and Judicial Watch had filed lawsuits using a federal law called the Freedom of Information Act (FOIA). The lawsuits by these civil rights organizations resulted in the release of thousands of pages of documents that described interrogation of prisoners by the Federal Bureau of Investigation (FBI), the U.S. Department of Defense, and the CIA.

Surely, government officials would prefer to keep secret the controversial actions of CIA agents and disputes between federal agencies. Yet the principle that U.S. citizens have a right to know about their government's actions is strong enough to expose the information for public scrutiny. Author Ellen M. Katz explains it this way:

> The heart of American democracy—and of any democracy—is meaningful, active participation by its people in government decisions that touch their lives.
>
> The soul of such a system is the ability of ordinary citizens to hold government officials accountable for their actions. Known as "transparency," this essential democratic process takes many forms, but all allow concerned citizens to see openly into the activities of their government, rather than permitting these processes to be cloaked in secrecy.[2]

In the United States, the concept of a transparent government, or open government, dates to the founding of the nation.

Government Transparency: A Tradition in the United States

In Great Britain in the seventeenth and eighteenth centuries, the government banned members of the press from reporting on the actions of legislators in Parliament. A reporter who ignored the ban faced a fine and even imprisonment.

The idea that a government should manage information took root in the British colonies in America. By the mid-1700s, an attitude had spread that British control of the colonies went hand in hand with a managed press and an ignorant public. In 1765, John Adams, one of the Founding Fathers and later the second president of the United States, wrote an essay in which he stated that "wherever a general knowledge and sensibility have prevailed among the people, arbitrary government and every kind of oppression have lessened and disappeared in proportion."[3] The public began to participate in the politics of colonial governments. Reporters were allowed to view debates between politicians in legislatures.

Following the American Revolutionary War (1775–1783), a question arose during debates about the proposed U.S. Constitution: Should Congress keep its proceedings secret, as the British Parliament had done? In June 1788, Patrick Henry expressed his view on government secrecy.

> The liberties of a people never were nor ever will be secure, when the transactions of their rulers may be concealed from them. The most iniquitous plots may

QUOTABLE

Louis D. Brandeis, U.S. Supreme Court Justice

Before Brandeis joined the Supreme Court, he used his position as an attorney to promote economic and social justice. He was especially concerned about secretive financial and banking practices that disadvantaged the average American. He once remarked that "Publicity is justly commended as a remedy for social and industrial diseases. Sunlight is said to be the best of disinfectants; electric light the most efficient policeman."*

* Louis D. Brandeis, *Other People's Money and How the Bankers Use It* (New York: Frederick A. Stokes, 1914), p. 92.

be carried on against their liberty and happiness. I am not an advocate for divulging indiscriminately all the operations of government, though the practice of our ancestors in some degree justifies it.[4]

An open government was soon established. When the U.S. House of Representatives first met, people watched the proceedings from a public gallery. Five years later, the Senate offered its own gallery for members of the public.

QUOTABLE

Benjamin Botts, Attorney for Aaron Burr

In 1807, Aaron Burr, who had served as vice president during President Thomas Jefferson's first term, was tried for treason. Burr's lawyers battled government lawyers for documents that supposedly proved Burr's treasonous acts. Eventually, the government released portions of the documents. Benjamin Botts, one of Burr's attorneys, expressed outrage about the concealment.

> I can never express in terms sufficiently strong, that detestation and abhorrence which every American should feel towards a system of state secrecy.... In a government of responsibility like ours, where all agents of the public must be responsible for their conduct, there can be but few secrets. The people of the United States have a right to know every public act, every thing that is done in the public way by their public functionaries. They ought to know the particulars of public transactions in all their bearings and relations, so as to be able to distinguish whether, and how far, they are conducted with fidelity and ability; and, with the exception of what relates to negotiations with foreign nations, or what is called the diplomatic department, there ought to be nothing suppressed or concealed.*

Botts promoted a philosophy of a transparent government that has not changed in 200 years.

* David Robertson, *Reports of the Trials of Colonel Aaron Burr for Treason and for a Misdemeanor* (Philadelphia: Hopkins and Earle, 1808), p. 517.

An Open-Government Tradition Becomes Law

Because the founders of the American republic were concerned that the government could become too powerful, they divided the U.S. government's power among three coequal branches. The legislative branch creates laws. It consists of the House of Representatives and the Senate, which form the U.S. Congress. The executive branch, headed by the president of the United States, implements and enforces laws written by Congress. The federal courts of the judicial branch interpret laws and apply laws to individual cases.

The actions of Congress and judicial proceedings are generally open to public scrutiny. By tradition, activities of the executive branch are relatively secret. During the Great Depression of the 1930s, the executive branch under the administration of President Franklin D. Roosevelt grew with the creation of federal regulatory agencies that wrote and enforced rules. These agencies had wide-ranging responsibilities that included providing funds to the disabled, the unemployed, and poor; protecting consumers from failing banks; and guarding stock investors from fraud. As an increasing number of federal agencies devised regulations that controlled American lives, the press wanted to know what went on behind the closed doors of those agencies.

The Second World War (1939–1945) brought increased secrecy of U.S. government actions and censorship of the news. The secrecy, however, did not end with the close of fighting. Hostility between the Soviet Union and the United States, and their allies, that occurred during the Cold War (1947–1991) fostered a continuation of wartime secrecy in the United States. The press objected and campaigned for an end of government information control. Even before the end of World War II, Kent Cooper, the executive director of the Associated Press, emphasized the need for an old freedom that he called the right to know. "The citizen is entitled to have access to news, fully and accurately presented," Cooper said. "There cannot be political freedom in one country, or in the world, without respect for 'the right to know.' "[5]

Yet fear of communism fueled the expansion of government secrecy. In 1951, President Harry Truman issued Executive Order 10290 so that every federal agency and department would have the authority to classify government information. This meant that nonmilitary federal agencies could withhold information from the public even in a time of peace. In 1954, President Dwight D. Eisenhower established the Office of Strategic Information. At the time, the government controlled information designated as "confidential," "secret," and "top secret." The Office of Strategic Information introduced a new type of controlled information: "unclassified strategic data" that a hostile foreign nation might use to harm the United States. Exactly what was this fourth type of censored data? Perhaps only Office of Strategic Information officials knew.

Government censorship frustrated not only the press; the executive branch refused to supply information to members of Congress. Bristling at this treatment, Representative John Moss of California, the chairman of the Special Subcommittee on Government Information, sent questionnaires to federal agencies about the types of information withheld from the public and asked what sort of authority they were claiming for concealing information. The responses revealed an arbitrary and deliberate culture of federal secrecy. Agency officials showed little concern for the public's interest in knowing about their government. A "right to know" is not spelled out in the U.S. Constitution, and no law at that time had granted one. Congress would have to draft legislation to create that right. The effort took more than 10 years.

As Moss, his colleagues, and members of the press continued their struggle to forge a more open government, Cold War fears spawned more concealment. "Secrecy labels were plastered on everything from innocuous academic articles to agency reports on wasteful spending," explains attorney Michael Lemov. "The reason often appeared to be to protect the agency from embarrassment, rather than protect legitimate government secrets."[6]

The Soviet Union accidentally helped efforts to pass a freedom of information law in the United States. On October 16, 1962, President John F. Kennedy saw photographs of Cuba that revealed Soviet nuclear ballistic missiles aimed at the United States. When the president returned unexpectedly from a trip, the White House initially informed the press that the president had returned because of a cold. It was only on October 22 that the president informed the nation about the missiles and that the United States had imposed a blockade on Cuba. For the week between these two dates, the White House kept the press largely in the dark while the country was on the brink of nuclear war. Finally, the Soviet Union removed the weapons, ending what came to be known as the Cuban Missile Crisis. The press complained about their treatment during this crucial time. Arthur Sylvester, assistant secretary of defense for public affairs in the Pentagon, admitted that the government had controlled and blocked the flow of news about the crisis. The government had an inherent right, Sylvester said, "to lie to save itself."[7] Sylvester's admissions sparked an uproar. It made people question the honesty of the government.

In June 1966, Moss moved to pass the Freedom of Information Act, which would protect the right of the public to information by amending the Administrative Procedure Act of 1946. Although the Administrative Procedure Act set up processes by which citizens could question federal regulation, it had been interpreted as giving agencies unlimited discretion to withhold records. A person who wanted to examine records in the possession of agencies and departments of the executive branch had to prove a need to know. A requestor also had to convince an agency that he or she was "properly and directly concerned" with the requested material. An agency's denial of a request ended the matter; a person had no remedy to appeal the decision.

Moss said the Freedom of Information Act would make three major changes in the law:

- The bill would ensure that the great majority of records would be available to "any person," not just those "properly and directly concerned."

- The bill would abolish the Administrative Procedure Act's vague standards for withholding information. Instead, the Freedom of Information Act listed nine categories of federal documents that agencies may withhold, such as national security information and law enforcement records. Agencies had to justify the decision not to disclose information that fell within the categories.

- For the first time, a citizen would have a remedy if an agency refused to provide requested information: The person could appeal to a U.S. district court.

The Freedom of Information Act would create a presumption that records are accessible to members of the public. This meant that the government would have the burden of showing that a record should not be made accessible to the public. The bill reversed policy: The "need to know" would be replaced by the "right to know." Moss argued that the Constitution recognized this right to information by guaranteeing free speech and a free press. "Inherent in the right of free speech and of free press is the right to know," Moss said. "It is our solemn responsibility as inheritors of the cause to do all in our power to strengthen those rights—to give them meaning."[8]

After Congress passed the Freedom of Information Act, President Lyndon B. Johnson signed the legislation into law on July 4, 1966. According to journalist Bill Moyers, who served as Johnson's press secretary, the president approved the act with little enthusiasm:

> [W]hat few people knew at the time is that LBJ had to be dragged kicking and screaming to the signing ceremony. He hated the very idea of the Freedom of Information Act; hated the thought of journalists rummaging in government closets; hated them challenging the official view of reality. He dug in his heels and even threatened

Using the Freedom of Information Act

Federal law entitles anyone to request a copy of any record from any agency in the executive branch, except for presidential records and nine exempted types of information; how to make a Freedom of Information Act (FOIA) request:

Before beginning: Locate appropriate official and make an informal request for the record

Written request

1. Write letter to agency's FOIA officer requesting record

2. "Reasonably describe" record; file or docket number not necessary

3. Be persistent; follow up frequently with agency officer

You can request
• Papers
• Reports
• Letters
• Films
• Computer tapes
• Photographs
• Sound recordings
• E-mails

For more information online: http://www.rcfp.org/foiact/index.html

Agency's response

■ Agency has 20 working days to release records or they can delay or deny the release of records based on exemptions within the law

■ May in some cases get extra time

■ May charge "reasonable" search fee, about $11 to $28 an hour; it may be reduced or waived

Exempted categories
• National security
• Personnel documents
• Records exempted by law
• Trade, commercial secrets
• Internal agency messages
• Officials' personal records
• Criminal investigations
• Federally regulated banks
• Oil and gas wells

For government help filing a request, call (202) 514-3642

 If request is **GRANTED**

 If request is **DELAYED**

 If request is **DENIED**

	Agency sends you copies requested	... if agency does not answer letter within 20 working days	... if agency withholds some or all information
You may file appeal ... Agency's FOI appeals officer handles appeal		YES	YES
You may file lawsuit in federal district court ... If you win, judge orders agency to supply information, may award you legal fees		YES	YES If appeal is denied

Source: Reporters Committee for Freedom of the Press

© 2009 MCT

The Freedom of Information Act was signed into law by President Lyndon B. Johnson on July 4, 1966, and went into effect the following year. In 1996, President Bill Clinton signed the Electronic Freedom of Information Act Amendments. This 2009 graphic outlines how a person may obtain government records using the Freedom of Information Act.

to pocket veto the bill after it reached the White House. Only the courage and political skill of a Congressman named John Moss got the bill passed at all, and that was after a twelve-year battle against his elders in Congress who blinked every time the sun shined in the dark corridors of power.[9]

Modifications of the Freedom of Information Act

During the early 1970s, Congress learned that federal agencies had been resisting the Freedom of Information Act. Agencies delayed responses to record requests, charged high prices for searching and copying documents, and used a contamination scheme to block those who requested records. Agencies would add confidential documents to a folder containing documents that should have been available to the public. Then they would refuse to spend the time required to sort the documents. To get the law to work, people had to pay for expensive lawsuits against agencies that refused to provide requested documents. Even that might not help. Suppose, for example, that an agency refused to release a document on the grounds that the information fell within the national security exemption. In *EPA v. Mink* (1973), the U.S. Supreme Court ruled that, in such a case, a judge could not review the document in private. A judge could determine only whether the agency had stamped the document as "classified." Federal agencies, not the courts, decided whether a document had been properly deemed to contain classified data.

In 1974, Congress fixed many of the act's problems with time limits for responding to a document request, fee limits, and rules on separating different types of documents. Congress also gave judges the authority to review classified documents to determine whether they had been rated "classified" merely to shield information for political purposes.

Congress has continued to fine-tune the Freedom of Information Act over the years. For example, the Electronic Freedom of Information Act Amendments of 1996 required that agencies make information available electronically. Some agencies make documents that are likely to generate interest easily available to anyone. For example, the FBI makes its well-known case files available in its "reading room" at http://vault.fbi.gov/. The amendments of the OPEN Government Act of 2007 recognized a new type of news media requester entitled to reduced fees: bloggers and writers who publish on Web sites. It is likely that Congress will continue to adapt the Freedom of Information Act to the changing times.

Different presidents have maintained varying policies for disclosing information under FOIA. In 1982, President Ronald Reagan issued an executive order that allowed federal agencies to hold back huge amounts of information under the national security exemption. Beginning in 1993, President Bill Clinton issued executive orders and memos to federal agencies to increase the effectiveness of the Freedom of Information Act. After the 9/11 terrorist attacks, George W. Bush's administration reduced the government's information disclosures. In fact, a memo issued by Attorney General John Ashcroft flipped the presumption of the Freedom of Information Act in favor of withholding information. Senator Patrick Leahy of Vermont protested this policy change. "The new policy says, in effect, 'When in doubt, don't disclose, and the Justice Department will support your denials in court,'" Leahy said. "It undermines FOIA's purpose, which is to facilitate the public's right to know the facts, not the government's ability to hide them."[10]

In 2009, President Barack Obama again reversed policy. "The Freedom of Information Act should be administered with a clear presumption: In the face of doubt, openness prevails," Obama stated in a memo. "The Government should not keep information confidential merely because public officials might be embarrassed by disclosure, because errors and failures might be revealed, or because of speculative or abstract fears."[11]

Freedom of Information Throughout the Country and Abroad

The Freedom of Information Act applies to records held by executive branch departments and agencies. It is not the only

OPEN Government Act of 2007

On December 31, 2007, President George W. Bush signed the OPEN Government Act of 2007 into law. In the act's preamble, Congress explained basic principles behind freedom of information laws:

Congress finds that—

(1) the Freedom of Information Act was signed into law on July 4, 1966, because the American people believe that—

(A) our constitutional democracy, our system of self-government, and our commitment to popular sovereignty depends upon the consent of the governed;

(B) such consent is not meaningful unless it is informed consent; and

(C) as Justice Black noted in his concurring opinion in *Barr v. Matteo* (360 U.S. 564 [1959]), "The effective functioning of a free government like ours depends largely on the force of an informed public opinion. This calls for the widest possible understanding of the quality of government service rendered by all elective or appointed public officials or employees.";

(2) the American people firmly believe that our system of government must itself be governed by a presumption of openness;

(3) the Freedom of Information Act establishes a "strong presumption in favor of disclosure" as noted by the United States Supreme Court in *United States Department of State v. Ray* (502 U.S. 164 [1991]), a presumption that applies to all agencies governed by that Act;

(4) "disclosure, not secrecy, is the dominant objective of the Act," as noted by the United States Supreme Court in *Department of Air Force v. Rose* (425 U.S. 352 [1976]);

(5) in practice, the Freedom of Information Act has not always lived up to the ideals of that Act; and

(6) Congress should regularly review section 552 of title 5, United States Code (commonly referred to as the Freedom of Information Act), in order to determine whether further changes and improvements are necessary to ensure that the Government remains open and accessible to the American people and is always based not upon the "need to know" but upon the fundamental "right to know."

Source: Public Law 110-175.

law that promotes transparency in the federal government. The Privacy Act enables U.S. citizens to access records held by most federal agencies if the records can be retrieved with personal information, such as the requesting citizen's name or Social Security number. Other laws allow the public to watch government meetings. For example, the Federal Advisory Committee Act and the Government in the Sunshine Act require that federal agencies and federal advisory committees serving the executive branch must be open to public observation. In addition, the Obama administration has created various initiatives to offer federal government information on the Internet.

These efforts, however, do not allow public access to information held by state and local governments. States have their own versions of freedom of information laws, called open-records laws, open-meetings laws, open-government laws, or sunshine laws. Whether the laws are effective is open for debate. A 2008 study by the Better Government Association and the National Freedom of Information Coalition concluded that state laws provide a haphazard way for the public to access government records. In fact, 38 of the 50 states received an "F" grade for effectiveness in responding to freedom of information requests. Like the Freedom of Information Act, state laws are works in progress.

The United States is not the only country to enact freedom of information laws. Perhaps the first such law was passed in Sweden in 1766. By 2006, about 70 countries had enacted freedom of information laws. More than half of these laws had been passed in the past 10 years, showing a trend toward open-government policies.

Just How Free Should Government Information Be?

In the wake of the Cuban Missile Crisis, an editorial in the *New York Times* highlighted the danger of government-controlled information:

> There is no doubt that "management" or "control" of the news is censorship described by a sweeter term.

Obama Administration Intensifies Sunlight on Government Functions

During January 2010, OMB Watch hosted a webcast on government transparency. One of the panelists, Ellen Miller, was executive director of the Sunlight Foundation, a nonprofit organization focused on the digitization of government data and the creation of Web sites to promote accessibility of that data. Miller praised efforts by the Obama administration:

> I think [the President] has begun to make a significant change in the culture of what openness means and move the default of where government information is from being in the hands of government into citizens' hands. In the 21st century, given new technology, things are no longer considered public by anyone unless they are online. I think the Administration has clearly endorsed that sort of fundamental cultural shift in information and transparency.... This is a sea change in my decades of experience of Washington.[*]

In a blog report about the OMB Watch program, Norm Eisen, special counsel to the president for ethics and government reform, described initiatives to increase government transparency.

> Our release of the White House visitor logs that the panelists applauded is only one example of the many steps the President has taken so far to increase government transparency. The Administration's other concrete commitments to openness include issuing the Open Government Directive, putting up more government information than ever before on data.gov and recovery.gov, reforming the government's FOIA [Freedom of Information Act] processes, providing on-line access to White House staff financial reports and salaries, issuing an executive order to fight unnecessary secrecy and speed declassification, reversing an executive order that previously limited access to presidential records, and webcasting White House meetings and conferences.[**]

[*] Policymaking for Open Government: An Assessment of the Obama Administration's First-Year Progress," OMB Watch Web site, January 28, 2010. http://www.ombwatch.org/webcastarchive.

[**] Norm Eisen, "More Praise on Transparency from the Experts," The White House Blog, February 5, 2010. http://www.whitehouse.gov/blog/2010/02/05/more-praise-transparency-experts.

There is no doubt that it restricts the people's right to know. There is no doubt that public positions upon great national issues cannot be intelligently formed unless the facts are available. There is no doubt that a democratic government cannot work if news of and about that government is long suppressed or managed or manipulated or controlled.[12]

Yet the author also warned that the government must withhold certain information during times of crisis. What sort of crisis justifies censorship? What types of information must be withheld? Who should decide what the public can know? Even in the absence of a crisis, how much information should flow from the government to its people? To what extent should the general public have access to the vast amount of private data on individuals stored in federal agencies? What is the proper balance between the public's right to know and the need of the government to protect certain information?

An Open Government Infringes Privacy Rights

For most of its history, the Social Security Administration (SSA) had a privacy policy that prohibited the sharing of a person's confidential data with law enforcement officials unless that person had been indicted or convicted of a crime. Documents obtained through a Freedom of Information Act request by the Electronic Privacy Information Center revealed that the agency changed its procedures after the terrorist attacks of September 11, 2001. Social Security officials agreed to an ad hoc, or informal, policy that authorized the release of confidential information, such as home addresses and medical data, to the FBI for investigations related to terrorism suspects.

Marcia Hofmann, the director of the Open Government Project at the Electronic Privacy Information Center, admitted that it was important for the FBI to obtain information required to prevent terrorism. "But an ad hoc policy like this is so broad that it allows law enforcement to obtain really sensitive information by merely claiming that the information is relevant to the 9/11 investigation," Hofmann told the *New York Times*. "There appears to be very little oversight."[1]

Consider this: A disclosure of confidential information from one government agency to another government agency sparked a controversy about the invasion of privacy. What would happen if the U.S. government became a truly open government that allowed the general public to access confidential information about U.S. citizens readily? What would happen to citizens' sense of privacy?

Americans have valued their privacy since the birth of the nation.

Americans consider the right to privacy to be a fundamental value. Lawyer Frederick S. Lane explains:

> At its core, the history of America *is* the history of the right to privacy. The myriad immigrants who have come to these shores, from the Pilgrims forward, have been motivated by many factors in their decision to come to the New World, but above all by that quintessential manifestation of privacy: the freedom to make up one's own mind about fundamental human issues, including religion, marriage, politics, employment, and education.[2]

The right to privacy has many aspects. For instance, a right to privacy can refer to the limits that society has on a person's activities. That is, people should be free from intrusion into their lives and property. In an 1834 copyright case, the U.S. Supreme Court acknowledged that "[t]he defendant asks nothing—wants nothing, but to be let alone until it can be shown that he has violated the rights of another."[3] About 60 years later, Samuel Warren and future U.S. Supreme Court justice Louis D. Brandeis argued for the "general right of the individual to be let alone."[4]

Another aspect of privacy is the right to maintain the confidentiality of personal information. For instance, people want privacy in their communications. Benjamin Franklin and William Hunter addressed this concern in 1753 when the British government appointed them to be deputy postmasters general of the colonies and run the Parliamentary Post. Franklin and Hunter ordered local postmasters to separate their post offices from their homes, a practice intended to decrease the risk that an unauthorized person would riffle through the mail. Other measures that aimed to ensure privacy included the transport of letters in sealed mailbags, and the requirement that a person who wanted to retrieve a posted letter had to provide proof of identification.

J. Holbrook, a special agent of the Post Office Department during the late nineteenth century, expressed an insider's opinion about the importance of privacy in communications:

> The laws of the land are intended not only to preserve the person and material property of every citizen sacred from intrusion, but to secure the privacy of his thoughts, so far as he sees fit to withhold them from others. Silence is as great a privilege as speech, and it is as important that every one should be able to maintain it whenever he pleases, as that he should be at liberty to utter his thoughts without restraint. Now the post-office undertakes to maintain this principle with regard to written communications as they are conveyed from one person to another through the mails. However unimportant the contents of a letter may be, the violation of its secrecy while in charge of the Post-Office Department, or even after having left its custody, becomes an offence of serious magnitude in the eye of the law.[5]

Concerns about information privacy also arise when the government collects and uses personal data. The U.S. Constitution sparked one of the earliest American controversies

In his novel *1984*, first published in 1949, George Orwell imagined a future in which a totalitarian government, called Big Brother, monitors every aspect of its citizens' lives through the collection and manipulation of information. Orwell is seen here being carefully monitored by Big Brother.

about information privacy by establishing proportional representation. The U.S. Constitution established a House of Representatives that would have members allocated by size of a state's population. As a result of this requirement, the United States became the first country to regularly count its citizens to maintain government structure. As secretary of state, Thomas Jefferson supervised the first census in 1790. Although it consisted of only six questions, these were sufficient to trigger resistance to the data collection. On August 24, 1790, Vermont census taker Roger Waite described this opposition to his superior. "Sir: I beg to report that I have been dogbit, goose-pecked, cowkicked, briar-scratched, shot at, and called by every 'fowel' name that can be tho't of," Waite said. "I have worked 12 days and made $2.00. I have had enough and I beg to resign my position as a census taker for Crittenden Township."[6]

Early census questionnaires focused on the head of a household. During the nineteenth century, Congress required that all free persons would provide information for the questionnaire, including questions about health, employment, income, education, and the value of owned real estate. This increased intrusion into private life incited widespread protests. An 1875 editorial shows the continuing resentment faced by census takers:

> "Be you a census man?" asked a frontiersman of a wandering tourist, who passed along a trail with a sketchbook under his arm. "Because if you be," he added by way of explanation, "I've got a big dog chained up behind the house; just say the word, and I'll let her loose." This rough welcome is a fair example of the esteem in which the census-taker is everywhere held. . . . The true-born freeman resents nothing more bitterly than any suspected invasion of his domestic privacy.[7]

The government stores huge amounts of private data.

The census was just the start of government programs for collecting personal data. During the early twentieth century, state and local governments collected increasing amounts of personal information about residents. Government records stored countless details about a person's life, from birth to death. Beginning in the 1930s, the federal government rapidly

Accessing the Databanks of "Big Brother"

George Orwell's novel *Nineteen Eighty-Four* (1949) takes place in a totalitarian society that does not tolerate privacy. Led by Big Brother, the government scrutinizes every aspect of the daily lives of its citizens, even their thoughts. By the early 1980s, advances in information technology inspired marketing executive Charles E. Rodgers to wonder whether American society was spiraling toward Orwell's nightmare world of 1984. At the time, he remarked:

> The year 1984 is but 33 months away. That we could realize, in three years, the loss of privacy described in *1984* is impossible. However, the fact remains that we have already been subjected to extraordinary invasions into our private lives by government and industry.
>
> How could this have happened? Because our benefactor, our "Big Brother" has been very busy. He has been able to invade our once-inviolate areas of privacy with frightening success. Let's face it. Each year we have been compelled to disclose more and more personal data to this ubiquitous guardian. Many of us do not realize fully the inroads this faceless character has made in our private lives. But he has made them.

Many agencies and organizations operate databanks that store personal information, Rodgers explained. Unauthorized access to this data is not only possible, but had been achieved by "schoolboys in a New York prep school." The key to extracting confidential data is the Social Security number. He noted:

> "Big Brother" has everyone's Social Security number. . . . "Big Brother" could plug into the system and ask data banks the country over for whatever information they may have on, say, Jonathan Livingston Seagull having the Social Security number of, say, 234-56-7890. That is all he would have to do. The dumb computers would respond immediately without thinking.

Source: Charles E. Rodgers Jr., " 'Big Brother' Is Racing '1984' Deadline," *New York Times*, March 22, 1981. http://www.nytimes.com/1981/03/22/nyregion/big-brother-is-racing-1984-deadline.html.

expanded. A mushrooming bureaucracy escalated the gathering of personal information about U.S. citizens. Today, government records contain a wealth of information about an individual. Law professor Daniel J. Solove offers a brief overview of the types of information found in government records:

> These records contain personal information including a person's physical description (age, photograph, height, weight, eye color); race, nationality, and gender; family life (children, marital history, divorces, and even intimate details about one's marital relationship); residence, location, and contact information (address, telephone number, value and type of property owned, description of one's home); political activity (political party affiliation, contributions to political groups, frequency of voting); financial condition (bankruptcies, financial information, salary, debts); employment (place of employment, job position, salary, sick leave); criminal history (arrests, convictions, traffic citations); health and medical condition (doctors' reports, psychiatrists' notes, drug prescriptions, diseases and other disorders); and identifying information (mother's maiden name, Social Security number). This list is far from complete.[8]

The types of government records include the so-called vital records—certificates that record birth, marriage, divorce, and death—and records that document the many interactions between a citizen and the local, state, and federal governments. Consider the driver's license. In California, for example, the Department of Motor Vehicles driver's license file includes:

- The driver's name
- Birth date
- Home and mailing addresses

- License number

- Physical description of the driver

- The driver's Social Security number

- Failures to appear in court and to pay traffic fines

- License status

- Information about traffic convictions

Voting records can include data about a person's place and date of birth, contact information, party affiliation, and even

Librarians Protest Invasion of Privacy

"What you do in the library—what you read, what you access, what you research—is nobody's business but yours," declared Judith Krug, director of the Office for Intellectual Freedom of the American Library Association (ALA).[*]

Librarians protested provisions of the Patriot Act. Enacted in the wake of the September 2001 terrorist attacks, the Patriot Act authorizes government agents to examine records of library reading lists and reference materials of patrons that the agents are investigating. The Electronic Privacy Information Center fueled the protest after it submitted a Freedom of Information Act request that uncovered e-mail messages between FBI agents who complained about "radical, militant librarians." The news inspired Krug to offer "Radical Militant Librarians" buttons at an ALA convention. The buttons, a big hit at the conference, injected a note of levity into a serious struggle. The ALA emphasizes the importance of this privacy issue:

> Protecting patron privacy and the confidentiality of library records are deep and longstanding principles of librarianship that guide the ALA's legislative and policy activities on privacy and surveillance issues. The freedom to read is an inherently important part of our First Amendment rights and civil liberties.[**]

[*] Amy Dorsett, "Librarians Would Shelve Patriot Act," *San Antonio Express-News*, January 25, 2006.
[**] American Library Association Web site, The USA PATRIOT Act. http://www.ala.org/ala/issuesadvocacy/advocacy/federallegislation/theusapatriotact/index.cfm.

Social Security number. A record of a court proceeding may contain a person's medical history, employment, lifestyle, Social Security number, and financial history. Other government records that contain personal information include employment records, property ownership records, Medicare records, federal and state tax records, school records, public library records, military records, and immigration records.

Free access to government records causes harm.

Government data warehouses store information that individuals consider private. If the general public could readily access this information, the loss of privacy would be profound. The American Library Association emphasizes that an invasion of privacy threatens core values:

Is Privacy Fading or Has It Vanished?

Daniel Solove, an expert in privacy and the law, underlines concerns about ready access to government records:

> Imagine that the government had the power to compel individuals to reveal a vast amount of personal information about themselves—where they live, their phone numbers, their physical description, their photograph, their age, their medical problems, all of their legal transgressions throughout their lifetimes whether serious crimes or minor infractions, the names of their parents, children, and spouses, their political party affiliations, where they work and what they do, the property that they own and its value, and sometimes even their psychotherapists' notes, doctors' records, and financial information.
>
> Then imagine that the government routinely poured this information into the public domain—by posting it on the Internet where it could be accessed from all over the world, by giving it away to any individual or company that asked for it, or even by providing entire databases of personal information upon request. In an increasingly "wired" society, with technology such as sophisticated computers to store, transfer, search, and sort through all this information, imagine the way that the information could be combined or used to obtain even more personal information.

When the right to privacy is eroded or stripped away, people are more likely to abandon or curtail their exploration of unpopular and unorthodox points of view. This chilling effect puts the intellectual development of our citizenry at risk. The very character of the American mind, which is premised on open inquiry, is thereby robbed of the free flow of ideas that makes innovation possible.[9]

Open access to government records also creates specific harms. These records store data, such as a person's Social Security number and mother's maiden name, which in turn can be used to access more confidential information, or to achieve identity theft. Identity theft occurs when someone uses

Imagine the ease with which this information could fall into the hands of crafty criminals, identity thieves, stalkers, and others who could use the information to threaten or intimidate individuals....

Imagine as well that this information would be traded among hundreds of private-sector companies that would combine it with a host of other information such as one's hobbies, purchases, magazines, organizations, credit history, and so on. This expanded profile would then be sold back to the government in order to investigate and monitor individuals more efficiently.

Stop imagining. What I described is what is currently beginning to occur throughout the United States by the use of federal, state, and local public records, and the threat posed to privacy by public records is rapidly becoming worse.[*]

Has information technology just begun to erode privacy, or has it ground privacy into dust? "You already have zero privacy. Get over it," said Scott G. McNealy, co-founder of Sun Microsystems.[**]

[*] Daniel J. Solove, "Access and Aggregation: Public Records, Privacy and the Constitution," *Minnesota Law Review* 86, No. 6 (2002), pp. 1138–1139.

[**] Edward C. Baig, Marcia Stepanek, and Neil Gross, "The Internet Wants Your Personal Info. What's in It for You?" *BusinessWeek*, April 5, 1999. http://www.businessweek.com/1999/99_14/b3623028.htm.

another individual's personally identifying information, without permission, to commit fraud or other crimes. The Federal Trade Commission estimates that as many as 9 million Americans have their identities stolen every year. Experts consider the Social Security number to be the key to identity theft. Many government agencies use the number as an identifier and store the information in their records.

Identity thieves wreak havoc with people's lives. Using their victim's name, they can hijack a credit card account or open a new account in an innocent person's name; open a bank account under another name and write bad checks; or start cellular or long-distance telephone service or a utility service. In short, when identity thieves purchase goods and services in their victim's name and do not pay the bills, they destroy that person's credit history. Victims can find that they cannot purchase an automobile on credit, rent an apartment, or finance a home. They can also discover a loss of employment opportunities. To reclaim their lives, victims of identity theft must clear their credit report. This essential process can require significant amounts of time and money.

Public access to personal information in court records creates other problems. An identity thief can use an innocent person's identifying information, linking the victim of identity theft to a crime, a mistake that becomes recorded in government documents and harms the victim's reputation. Witnesses identified in court records risk retribution for testifying against criminal defendants. According to the Privacy Rights Clearinghouse, an expert in domestic violence cases stated that many victims of stalking refuse to file cases in court because they fear that the stalker will use their private information to find them and harm them.

Summary

While a transparent government would allow U.S. citizens to scrutinize the workings of their government and its agents, unrestrained transparency would also enable the public to examine the massive amounts of private information collected and stockpiled by local, state, and federal governments. Americans consider privacy to be a fundamental value. The breach of privacy resulting from free access to government records would threaten the reputations, livelihoods, and the lives of American citizens.

Laws and Courts
Safeguard Privacy

Does a police officer have privacy rights in his text messages sent via a government-issued pager? In California, the Ontario Police Department distributed pagers to its SWAT team, so that SWAT officers could send and receive messages related to their duties. Officers could also use their pagers for a limited number of personal messages. The pagers, issued by Arch Wireless Operating Company, worked like this: A pager sent a message via a radio frequency transmission to an Arch Wireless receiving station. The message eventually entered into the Arch Wireless computer network and then into the Arch Wireless computer server. The server archived a copy of the message and stored a second copy in the server system until the recipient pager was ready to accept delivery of the text message.

The police department decided to audit text messages to determine whether officers had been sending too many personal messages with their pagers. Arch Wireless made copies of archived text messages and forwarded them to the police chief. During the course of the review, the police chief read transcripts of intimate messages sent by Sergeant Jeff Quon of the SWAT team.

Quon sued the city of Ontario, the police department, and the police chief for violating his privacy rights, as protected by the Fourth Amendment of the U.S. Constitution and the California Constitution. The Fourth Amendment protects the "right of the people to be secure in their persons, houses, papers, and effects, against unreasonable searches and seizures." The California Constitution asserts that "[a]ll people are by nature free and independent and have inalienable rights. Among these are enjoying and defending life and liberty, acquiring, possessing, and protecting property, and pursuing and obtaining safety, happiness, and privacy."[1] Quon also alleged that Arch Wireless had violated the Stored Communications Act by sending the archived records of text messages. The Stored Communications Act forbids providers of communication services from revealing private communications to certain individuals.

After losing his case in a U.S. district court, Quon appealed the decision. The U.S. Court of Appeals for the Ninth Circuit reversed that decision, and this time, the city of Ontario and the other defendants appealed. The U.S. Supreme Court found a way to resolve the case without delving into the question about an employee's privacy expectations in messages sent on a device provided by the employer. In the 2010 case of *City of Ontario v. Quon*, the U.S. Supreme Court chose not to examine the question of whether Quon had a reasonable expectation of privacy in his pager messages because the Court found that the city had acted reasonably in accessing his messages. (If he did have a reasonable expectation of privacy *and* the city had acted unreasonably, Quon would have had a case for a violation of his Fourth Amendment rights.) The Court avoided the privacy issue, because the law's treatment of workplace privacy norms is still evolving.

Nevertheless, *Quon v. Arch Wireless* shows the various resources that a person can use to fight an invasion of privacy, including the U.S. Constitution, a state constitution, and federal law.

Privacy laws prevent FOI laws from infringing on privacy rights.

The federal government and state governments have enacted many laws to protect personal information stored in government records. A good place to start looking for such protection is the Freedom of Information Act, the most significant of all freedom of information laws.

The FOIA created a presumption that members of the public can access government records. The act also established exemptions to this rule. Exemption 6 states that the law does not apply to personnel files, medical files, and similar files if the disclosure of the information would be an unwarranted invasion of personal privacy. Thanks to Exemption 6, courts have protected many types of personal information, such as names and home addresses of individuals, medical condition, marital status, family fights, legitimacy of children, welfare payments, birth dates, religious affiliations, Social Security numbers, and financial information.

Exemption 7C of the act protects personal data contained within records and information compiled for law enforcement purposes. Plaintiffs have used Exemption 7 to protect the names and addresses of witnesses who provided information to law enforcement agencies, the identities of law enforcement personnel referenced in investigatory files, and the names of people who just happened to be mentioned in law enforcement files.

Exemptions 6 and 7C protect against an *unwarranted* invasion of personal privacy. A court can decide whether an invasion of personal privacy is warranted in a particular case. Judges must balance the privacy interest compromised by disclosure against any public interest in the requested information.

THE LETTER OF THE LAW

Privacy Exemptions of the Freedom of Information Act

The Freedom of Information Act requires federal agencies to release information to the public. The act lists exceptions to this rule: Exemptions 4, 6, and 7 apply to government documents that contain personal or confidential information.

The Freedom of Information Act does not apply to matters that are:

(4) trade secrets and commercial or financial information obtained from a person and privileged or confidential; ...

(6) personnel and medical files and similar files the disclosure of which would constitute a clearly unwarranted invasion of personal privacy;

(7) records or information compiled for law enforcement purposes, but only to the extent that the production of such law enforcement records or information (A) could reasonably be expected to interfere with enforcement proceedings, (B) would deprive a person of a right to a fair trial or an impartial adjudication, (C) could reasonably be expected to constitute an unwarranted invasion of personal privacy, (D) could reasonably be expected to disclose the identity of a confidential source, including a State, local, or foreign agency or authority or any private institution which furnished information on a confidential basis, and, in the case of a record or information compiled by a criminal law enforcement authority in the course of a criminal investigation or by an agency conducting a lawful national security intelligence investigation, information furnished by a confidential source, (E) would disclose techniques and procedures for law enforcement investigations or prosecutions, or would disclose guidelines for law enforcement investigations or prosecutions if such disclosure could reasonably be expected to risk circumvention of the law, or (F) could reasonably be expected to endanger the life or physical safety of any individual.

Note that Exemption 4 pertains to confidential business information included in government records. Other statues and the common law protect such data as well.

Source: 5 U.S.C. §552.

Congress has enacted many other federal laws to protect personal information stored in records. The most significant privacy law is the Privacy Act of 1974, a statute partly inspired by the break-in at the Watergate office of the Democratic National Committee by operatives of the Nixon White House who wanted to install illegal listening devices. The U.S. Department of Justice described the main features of the Privacy Act:

> Broadly stated, the purpose of the Privacy Act is to balance the government's need to maintain information about individuals with the rights of individuals to be protected against unwarranted invasions of their privacy stemming from federal agencies' collection, maintenance, use, and disclosure of personal information about them. The historical context of the Act is important to an understanding of its remedial purposes. In 1974, Congress was concerned with curbing the illegal surveillance and investigation of individuals by federal agencies that had been exposed during the Watergate scandal. It was also concerned with potential abuses presented by the government's increasing use of computers to store and retrieve personal data by means of a universal identifier—such as an individual's social security number.[2]

Although the Privacy Act requires federal agencies to ensure the security and confidentiality of records, the law has exceptions that allow an agency to release an individual's private information without the consent of that individual. For example, a federal entity may release records to protect the safety or health of an individual, or upon the request by a law enforcement agency.

Other federal laws that protect privacy include the following:

- The Electronic Communications Privacy Act established that providers of electronic communications services must restrict access to the contents of stored computerized records. The act applies to telephone companies and Internet service providers, and covers subscriber information, transaction records, and the content of communications. The Stored Communications Act, mentioned in the *Quon v. Arch Wireless* case, is part of the Electronic Communications Privacy Act.

- The Mail Privacy Statute forbids a person from opening mail without a search warrant or the consent of the addressee.

- The Driver's Privacy Protection Act prohibits state departments of motor vehicles from disclosing personal data stored in driver's license files and motor vehicle registration records.

- The Health Insurance Portability and Accountability Act established a national standard for health care organizations to protect private information stored in electronic medical records. In addition to a patient's medical history, a medical record may include private information, such as laboratory test results, medical procedures, prescribed medications, family medical history, and information about a patient's lifestyle.

- The Genetic Information Nondiscrimination Act forbids insurers from denying coverage or charging higher premiums based solely on a genetic tendency to develop a disease in the future. The act also prohibits employers from basing an employment decision upon a job applicant's genetic information.

States have also created laws that provide additional privacy for its citizens. Some states have laws to restrict access to personal data stored in public records, as well as laws that try to limit marketing and other commercial uses of personal information obtained from public records. State legislatures have enacted privacy statutes such as:

- Freedom of information statutes with exemptions that allow state agencies to withhold information if disclosure would reveal certain types of personally identifiable information, such as Social Security numbers.

- School records statutes that restrict the disclosure of personal data in school records to third parties.

FROM THE BENCH

U.S. Department of State v. Ray, 502 U.S. 164 (1991)

In the early 1980s, President Ronald Reagan ordered the Coast Guard to intercept vessels carrying undocumented emigrants from Haiti and to return them to their point of origin unless they qualified for refugee status. The Haitian government assured the U.S. secretary of state that it would not prosecute Haitians returned to Haiti. To verify the safety of returned Haitians, U.S. State Department staff privately interviewed a number of the unsuccessful emigrants about six months after they had returned to their country. All but one or two reported that they had not been harassed or prosecuted.

Years later, a group wanted to prove that Haitians who immigrated illegally would face persecution if they returned to their homeland. They made a series of FOIA requests to government agencies for copies of the State Department interviews. The government provided documents but removed the names and other identifying information about the interviewed Haitians. The group filed a lawsuit to obtain the missing data.

When the matter reached the U.S. Supreme Court, the Court had to decide whether disclosure of the full interview reports would create a clearly unwarranted invasion of an interviewee's privacy. The answer required a balancing of the individual's right of privacy against the basic policy of opening agency action to the light of public scrutiny:

> As the Government points out, many of these summaries contain personal details about particular interviewees. Thus, if the summaries are released without the names redacted, highly personal information regarding marital and employment status, children, living conditions, and attempts to enter the United States would be linked publicly with particular, named individuals. Although disclosure of such personal information constitutes only a *de*

- Employment records statutes that forbid employers from gathering personal information about a job applicant, including gender, race, religion, and national origin.

- Criminal justice information statutes that require strict security procedures to protect personal information stored in criminal justice information systems.

minimis [i.e., trivial] invasion of privacy when the identities of the interviewees are unknown, the invasion of privacy becomes significant when the personal information is linked to particular interviewees.

In addition, disclosure of the unredacted interview summaries would publicly identify the interviewees as people who cooperated with a State Department investigation of the Haitian Government's compliance with its promise to the United States Government not to prosecute the returnees.... [T]his group of interviewees occupies a special status: They left their homeland in violation of Haitian law and are protected from prosecution by their government's assurance to the State Department. Although the Department's monitoring program indicates that that assurance has been fulfilled, it nevertheless remains true that the State Department considered the danger of mistreatment sufficiently real to necessitate that monitoring program. How significant the danger of mistreatment may now be is, of course, impossible to measure, but the privacy interest in protecting these individuals from any retaliatory action that might result from a renewed interest in their aborted attempts to emigrate must be given great weight. Indeed, the very purpose of respondents' [i.e., the original plaintiffs'] FOIA request is to attempt to prove that such a danger is present today....

In the Court's view, the public had a legitimate interest in knowing whether the State Department adequately monitored Haiti's compliance with its promise not to prosecute returnees. "We are persuaded, however," the Court wrote, "that this public interest has been adequately served by disclosure of the redacted interview summaries and that disclosure of the unredacted documents would therefore constitute a clearly unwarranted invasion of the interviewees' privacy."

- Bank records statutes that ban financial institutions from revealing a customer's financial records to a third party without the customer's consent or a court's approval.

- Prescription privacy laws that forbid the transfer or use of prescription information records for commercial purposes.

- Genetic privacy statutes that variously require a person's consent to disclose their genetic test results, prohibit insurers from denying or restricting coverage based on an individual's genetic test results, and forbid employers from requiring a job applicant to get a genetic test and from using genetic data to deny an individual employment.

Courts uphold the privacy rights of individuals.

Courts protect privacy rights granted by federal and state statutes. Courts also look to privacy protection in the common law, a collection of legal principles created by judges when they decide individual cases. In 1890, Samuel Warren and Louis D. Brandeis argued that U.S. courts should protect an individual's privacy:

> The common law secures to each individual the right of determining, ordinarily, to what extent his thoughts, sentiments, and emotions shall be communicated to others. Under our system of government, he can never be compelled to express them (except when upon the witness stand); and even if he has chosen to give them expression, he generally retains the power to fix the limits of the publicity which shall be given them. The existence of this right does not depend upon the particular method of expression adopted. It is immaterial whether it be by word or by signs, in painting, by sculpture, or in music. Neither does the existence of the right depend upon the nature or value of the thought

Louis D. Brandeis served as an associate justice of the United States Supreme Court from 1916 to 1939. Long before his career on the bench began, he helped develop the concept of a "right to privacy" in American law through an article he co-wrote for the *Harvard Law Review* in 1890.

or emotion, nor upon the excellence of the means of expression. The same protection is accorded to a casual letter or an entry in a diary and to the most valuable poem or essay, to a botch or daub and to a masterpiece. In every such case the individual is entitled to decide whether that which is his shall be given to the public. . . . [T]he common-law protection enables him to control absolutely the act of publication, and in the exercise of his own discretion, to decide whether there shall be any publication at all. (Footnotes omitted.)[3]

Warren and Brandeis argued that a person has a right to decide whether certain information should be made available to the public. Today, courts recognize various forms of common law privacy right violations, including the public disclosure of personal letters, private family matters, medical treatment, and other private facts. The existence of these privacy right violations discourages a person from invading another's privacy.

Although the U.S. Constitution lacks such *explicit* guarantees of personal privacy, the U.S. Supreme Court decided in 1965 that the Constitution has *implicit* guarantees of personal privacy—a person just needs to read between the lines. This 1965 case, *Griswold v. Connecticut*, concerned the constitutionality of a Connecticut statute that made it a crime for any person to use birth control or to offer advice on the use of contraceptives. The Supreme Court decided that the law was unconstitutional because it violated a right to privacy. Justice William O. Douglas explained that the amendments of the Constitution establish more rights than those listed:

The right of freedom of speech and press includes not only the right to utter or to print, but the right to distribute, the right to receive, the right to read and freedom of inquiry, freedom of thought, and freedom to teach—indeed, the freedom of the entire university community. Without those peripheral rights, the specific rights would be less secure. (Citations omitted.)[4]

FROM THE BENCH

Whalen v. Roe, 429 U.S. 589 (1977)

Legal scholars consider the *Griswold v. Connecticut* decision to protect the general right of an individual to be free of government intrusion. *Whalen v. Roe* indicates that the Supreme Court should recognize a constitutional right to privacy in the collection, storage, and distribution of data in government databases. The *Whalen* case concerned the constitutionality of a New York law that established a computer system to store the names and addresses of individuals who had been prescribed certain drugs that had both a lawful and an unlawful market. The Court ultimately decided that the government had a substantial interest in monitoring the use of such drugs. In this case, the law did not create an impermissible invasion of privacy. The Court acknowledged, however, that it might recognize the right to privacy as the right to control information:

> A final word about issues we have not decided. We are not unaware of the threat to privacy implicit in the accumulation of vast amounts of personal information in computerized data banks or other massive government files. The collection of taxes, the distribution of welfare and social security benefits, the supervision of public health, the direction of our Armed Forces, and the enforcement of the criminal laws all require the orderly preservation of great quantities of information, much of which is personal in character and potentially embarrassing or harmful if disclosed. The right to collect and use such data for public purposes is typically accompanied by a concomitant statutory or regulatory duty to avoid unwarranted disclosures. Recognizing that, in some circumstances, that duty arguably has its roots in the Constitution, nevertheless New York's statutory scheme, and its implementing administrative procedures, evidence a proper concern with, and protection of, the individual's interest in privacy. We therefore need not, and do not, decide any question which might be presented by the unwarranted disclosure of accumulated private data—whether intentional or unintentional—or by a system that did not contain comparable security provisions. (Footnote omitted.)

"[S]pecific guarantees in the Bill of Rights have penumbras formed by emanations from those guarantees that help give them life and substance," Douglas wrote. "Various guarantees create zones of privacy."[5] In other words, the Supreme Court said that implicit rights support the rights explicitly guaranteed by the Constitution. The right to privacy is one of these implicit rights that "emanate" from the explicit rights. At the time, some legal commentators found the Court's justification for a right to privacy bordering on the mystical. Yet *Griswold* inspired a series of privacy cases that protect individual privacy rights from intrusion by federal and state governments.

Summary

An open government does not mean that the public can or should have access to all the information stored in government records. In the United States, the purpose of freedom of information is to enable U.S. citizens to monitor their government, not to spy upon each other. The Freedom of Information Act itself establishes protections against invasions of privacy. Other federal and state statutes bolster these defenses. The U.S. Constitution, state constitutions, and common law grant privacy rights that complement rights endowed by statutory law. An open government does not threaten the privacy of individuals.

Protection of State Secrets Requires Strict Restrictions on FOI

In January 1991, Pentagon leaders predicted that the Persian Gulf War would not end in a quick victory for the United States. One problem facing the U.S. military was the inability to destroy Iraq's supply of Soviet-designed SS-1 missiles (code-named Scud missiles). The Iraqi dictator Saddam Hussein had devised tactics to hide his arsenal from U.S. intelligence. Years later, John Podesta, who served as President Bill Clinton's chief of staff from 1998 to 2001, said that the media had inadvertently caused the problem:

> In 1990, U.S. press reports disclosed that our imagery satellites had detected fixed Scud missile launch sites in western Iraq. Baghdad responded by building decoy launchers to fix our attention, and, during the early phases of the war, our air strikes, on these sites, which

51

they no longer intended to use. While our pilots risked their lives to attack the unused fixed positions, the Iraqis switched to using mobile Scud launchers, from which they rained missiles on Israel and Saudi Arabia.[1]

A government must keep secrets.

This incident highlights the danger of a truly open government, one in which the public can access any information that a government possesses. A government cannot operate effectively unless it guards state secrets, such as military and diplomatic information. Secrecy serves national security by:

- concealing information that can provide an advantage over an adversary;

- preventing an adversary from acquiring an advantage that could harm the United States;

- protecting the identities of those who risk their lives and their families to provide intelligence data.

Secrecy also is essential in maintaining surprise that can be critical for a successful military operation. Diplomatic negotiations often rely upon secrecy as well.

A U.S. Senate commission studied the problem of protecting government secrecy. "Greater openness permits more public understanding of the Government's actions and also makes it more possible for the Government to respond to criticism and justify those actions," the Commission on Protecting and Reducing Government Secrecy acknowledged.[2] Yet the commission agreed that the government must not divulge all information: "Certain types of information—for example, the identity of sources whose exposure would jeopardize human life, signals or imagery intelligence the loss of which would profoundly hinder the capability to collect critical data, or information that could aid terrorists—must be assiduously protected."[3]

Since 1940, U.S. presidents have protected much of this secret information with executive orders. These executive orders have established a classification system of data based on the degree of damage that could result from disclosure. If publicly revealed, "confidential" information is expected to damage national security. Serious damage is expected to result from the release of "secret" information, whereas disclosure of "top secret" information is expected to inflict exceptionally grave damage upon national security. The CIA, the Department of Energy, the Department of Defense, and other agencies use variations of the three-part classification scheme.

Executive orders are not the only way to protect government secrets. Congress enacts laws to guard against public exposure of

---

QUOTABLE

John Podesta, former White House chief of staff

According to John Podesta, the need for openness must be balanced with the need for appropriate secrecy:

> [O]ur drive for greater openness cannot be interpreted by anyone as a license to disclose classified information. There must be respect for the law, and respect for the reality that there are secrets worth protecting.
>
> Some information must be closely held to protect national security and to engage in effective diplomacy. And often our interest in protecting the method by which information was obtained is even greater than our interest in protecting its content. For example, when disclosures of classified information mention satellite photos, other nations often take heed and conceal their activities.
>
> When "intercepts" or "eavesdropping" are mentioned, we often find that codes or equipment are changed and listening devices are disabled. And when human sources are revealed ... the consequences can be fatal.

Source: John Podesta, "Remarks on Government Secrecy vs. Disclosure," The First Amendment Center, March 27, 1999. http://www.firstamendmentcenter.org//news.aspx?id=5631.

sensitive data, and the courts block the public from accessing information that can harm the country if exposed to the light of day.

Lawmakers and judges protect state secrets.

Exemption 1 of the Freedom of Information Act, the statute intended to provide an open government, protects state secrets. Originally, the exemption excluded information "specifically required by Executive Order to be kept secret in the interest of national defense or foreign policy." In its 1973 decision *EPA v. Mink*, the U.S. Supreme Court ruled that a judge could verify that a government agency had stamped a requested document as "classified," but could not review the contents of the document. A year later, Congress gave judges the authority to review classified documents to determine whether they had been properly rated "classified."

Although judges may assess classified data, they remain reluctant to order disclosure if the information might damage America's military defense or international relationships. Consider the 2006 case *American Civil Liberties Union v. Federal Bureau of Investigation*. The ACLU filed a FOIA lawsuit to obtain FBI documents about the agency's surveillance of certain U.S. political and religious organizations. The FBI produced some documents, but withheld others claiming Exemption 1. Did the FBI properly deny information? "[W]hile a court is ultimately to make its own decision, that decision must take seriously the government's predictions about the security implications of releasing particular information to the public," the judge wrote.[4] "[T]he court must recognize that the executive branch departments responsible for national security and national defense have unique insights and special expertise concerning the kind of disclosures that may be harmful."[5] For the majority of the withheld documents, the judge decided that

> the FBI has properly invoked Exemption 1 in order to protect against the disclosure of intelligence sources,

One of the most influential Founding Fathers, Thomas Jefferson authored the Declaration of Independence in 1776 and served as the third president of the United States from 1801 to 1809. He was also the first president to claim executive privilege, a power not specified in the U.S. Constitution.

operations, and methods; to prevent the publication of classified file numbers, numerical designators, and names of classified operational units; and to prevent the identification of counterintelligence targets, cooperating foreign governments, and foreign relations information.[6]

In another case, an attorney filed a FOIA lawsuit against the U.S. Department of Defense. The attorney wanted information about the capture of a Turkish citizen by the United States in Pakistan and that person's detention at the U.S. naval base at Guantánamo Bay, Cuba. The judge decided that Exemption 1 protects intelligence assessments and conclusions reached by analysts, because "disclosure would reveal how intelligence analysts evaluate intelligence information, what information they find credible and what information they discredit, and how they reach their intelligence conclusions."[7] The judge also decreed that the Department of Defense had properly withheld documents that would expose intelligence methods used by government personnel to assemble and coordinate intelligence data, and plans for future intelligence gathering.

The executive privilege, or state secrets privilege, is another mechanism used by the executive branch of the government to protect information from public disclosure. The privilege evolved from common law and allows government officials to resist a court-ordered release of information if disclosure would harm the military or foreign affairs. In the United States, the privilege dates at least to the time of President Thomas Jefferson, who asserted executive privilege during the 1807 treason trial of Aaron Burr.

In 1953, the U.S. Supreme Court described the modern version of the procedure that a court should use to evaluate a claim of state secrets privilege. *United States v. Reynolds* concerned civilians who died aboard a B-29 military aircraft. A fire broke out in one of the bomber's engines and the airplane crashed, killing six of the nine crewmembers, and three of the four civilian observers. The widows of the deceased civilian observers sued the government to obtain copies of the Air Force's accident-investigation report and statements made by surviving crew members during the investigation. The Air Force opposed disclosure of the documents, saying the aircraft and its occupants had been engaged in a mission to test secret electronic equipment. Disclosure of the records would impede national security, the Air Force insisted.

The Supreme Court said that, after the government asserts a claim of privilege, a court must decide whether the circumstances are appropriate for the claim of privilege *without* forcing the government to disclose the information. If a court decides that the government has properly claimed the privilege, it cannot force disclosure of the information. In *United States v. Reynolds*, the Court noted that new electronic devices had greatly enhanced the use of air power in national defense, and that these electronic devices must be kept secret so that the military could effectively use them to safeguard national interests. Finding a reasonable danger that the accident investigation report would contain references to the secret electronic equipment, the Court concluded that the Air Force had properly asserted the privilege and would not review the requested documents or compel the Air Force to give copies to the three widows.

The government must safeguard data beyond state secrets.

In the *Reynolds* case, the U.S. Supreme Court protected documents that may have described an electronics system for military aircraft. What about documents that describe components of such a system? An analyst of a foreign government could use information about the components to piece together a picture of the complete electronic system. If the government considers the electronic system to be a state secret, then the government should also conceal bits of data that could reveal the electronic system. This idea about protecting pieces of a puzzle is called the mosaic theory. As the U.S. Navy explains in its freedom of information regulations, the mosaic theory is the "concept that apparently harmless pieces of information when assembled together could reveal a damaging picture."[8]

Courts have used the mosaic theory to prevent disclosure of apparently innocuous data that may expose a state secret. The

QUOTABLE

Dick Cheney, former vice president of the United States

The group al-Qaeda inflicted terrorist attacks against New York City and Washington, D.C., on September 11, 2001, during the first year of the Bush administration. In May 2009, Cheney, who was vice president at the time of the 9/11 attacks, spoke about the continuing terrorist threat to the United States and the need for secrecy:

> Our government prevented attacks and saved lives through the Terrorist Surveillance Program, which let us intercept calls and track contacts between al-Qaeda operatives and persons inside the United States. The program was top secret, and for good reason, until the editors of the New York Times got it and put it on the front page. After 9/11, the Times had spent months publishing the pictures and the stories of everyone killed by al-Qaeda on 9/11. Now here was that same newspaper publishing secrets in a way that could only help al-Qaeda. It impressed the Pulitzer committee, but it damn sure didn't serve the interests of our country, or the safety of our people.

Cheney also addressed President Barack Obama's decision to release memos describing the CIA's harsh methods for interrogating al-Qaeda suspects in secret overseas prisons. "Releasing the interrogation memos was flatly contrary to the national security interest of the United States," he said. "The harm done only begins with top secret information now in the hands of the terrorists, who have just received a lengthy insert for their training manual."

Source: "Remarks by Richard B. Cheney," American Enterprise Institute, May 21, 2009. http://www.aei.org/speech/100050.

Supreme Court tackled the mosaic theory in *Central Intelligence Agency v. Sims* in 1985. The case began when attorney John C. Sims and Dr. Sidney M. Wolfe, the director of the Public Citizen Health Research Group, filed a FOIA request with the CIA for the names of the institutions and individuals that had performed research for a secret CIA-funded program, code-named MKULTRA. The CIA had set up the project to counter advances in brainwashing and interrogation techniques developed by the Soviet Union and the People's Republic of China. The Supreme Court agreed with the CIA's decision to protect the names of the researchers who had served as intelligence sources. The Court also agreed that disclosure of the researchers' institutions posed an unacceptable risk of revealing the identities of the researchers. The Court explained its mosaic theory reasoning, quoting conclusions made by other courts:

> [T]he very nature of the intelligence apparatus of any country is to try to find out the concerns of others; bits and pieces of data "may aid in piecing together bits of other information even when the individual piece is not of obvious importance in itself." Thus, "[w]hat may seem trivial to the uninformed may appear of great moment to one who has a broad view of the scene, and may put the questioned item of information in its proper context." Accordingly, the Director [of the CIA] . . . has power to withhold superficially innocuous information on the ground that it might enable an observer to discover the identity of an intelligence source. (Citations omitted.)[9]

Although the *Sims* case focused on CIA records, courts have applied the mosaic theory rationale to records held by other agencies, including records pertaining to the 9/11 terrorist attacks on the United States. On September 11, 2001, terrorists hijacked four commercial airliners, which crashed into the

Pentagon near Washington, D.C., into a field in Pennsylvania, and into the twin towers of the World Trade Center in New York City. This new war of terrorism aimed at military and civilian targets. Officials asserted that more information must remain secret to protect structures and systems owned by the private sector:

> [B]y far the most potent argument for massively expanding secrecy—and the one most transformative of public attitudes—is the one that arises out of the *sui generis* [i.e., unique] nature of the terrorist threat, directed as it is against a civilian population on American soil. The domestic aspect and the targeting of civilian infrastructure has radically redefined the debate about open government and allowed secrecy to migrate well beyond the traditional confines of the intelligence and military realm to Main Street, U.S.A.
>
> Today, . . . no aspect of ordinary life is seen to be exempt from the terrorists' crosshairs. More than any other single factor, this sense of ubiquitous vulnerability, that everything is considered part of the "critical infrastructure," has been the impetus for expanding the breadth and scope of secrecy.[10]

According to Representative J.C. Watts Jr. of Oklahoma, "85 percent of our critical infrastructure is owned by the private sector."[11] Individuals in the private sector have not routinely disclosed information about infrastructure vulnerabilities and capabilities. In response to the 9/11 attacks, Congress wrote the Critical Infrastructure Information Act of 2002 to encourage the private sector to share information with the Homeland Security Department, especially companies in transportation, computer systems, financial services, power-generating systems, and telecommunications. Government analysts use the information to identify vulnerabilities in the country's critical infrastructure, protect critical infrastructure, and improve recovery measures in the event of a disaster. The law covers a range of data, such as glitches in software programs used by the Department of Defense and possible leaks at a chemical plant. Information transferred from the private sector to the federal government is shielded from public access. The law created a new, broad exemption to protect information from FOIA and open-records laws of state and local governments.

Summary

To safeguard the security of the nation and to ensure the success of diplomatic negotiations, the U.S. government must keep certain secrets. Government agencies ensure confidentiality by classifying documents as secret. When necessary, the executive branch asserts the state secrets privilege. Judges respect these practices and typically defer to governmental expertise. Aware of the need to guard state secrets, Congress included an exemption, Exemption 1, in the Freedom of Information Act. To protect apparently innocuous data that could reveal a state secret, courts accept the mosaic theory. The War on Terror that began after the 9/11 attacks created the need for a new type of exemption from government transparency: private-sector data that may reveal vulnerabilities in the critical infrastructure of the nation.

After 9/11, in order to better protect the nation from future terrorist attacks, the Bush administration increased the number of documents classified as secret and pulled certain information from government Web sites. The measures aroused much criticism from open-government advocates. Yet during this time of enhanced secrecy, terrorists did not inflict another major attack within the United States. This shows the effectiveness of extended secrecy and the need to continue the policy.

Democracy Requires Inspection of State Secrets

"The problem is that all governments prefer to operate in secret—it is efficient and self-protective," says lawyer Ronald Goldfarb. "It hides mismanagement, bungling, and misconduct."[1] Government secrets also conceal information that may be used to save lives.

In April 2010, 29 miners died after an explosion at a coal mine in Montcoal, West Virginia. Three months earlier, a federal inspector had visited the mine and discovered that the air in part of the mine flowed in the wrong direction. Miners depended on correct airflow to prevent gases and coal dust from accumulating to explosive concentrations. Nevertheless, mine officials had assured the inspector that the problem was nothing to worry about. Although the company fixed the violation later that day, the inspector noted the company's casual attitude in his notebook.

The Mine Safety and Health Administration (MSHA) released the inspector's notes more than a week *after* the mine explosion. "This is life and death stuff," Steven Aftergood of the Federation of American Scientists told the *Huffington Post.* "And by withholding this information from the public domain, the government's capacity to spur corrective action was blocked."[2] Dan Froomkin, a reporter for the *Huffington Post*, wrote that the MSHA had been a model agency for disclosing information to the public "until the Bush administration dropped a gigantic veil of secrecy across all government agencies in the wake of the 9/11 terrorist attacks. Suddenly, MSHA wouldn't release even basic information about inspections and investigations."[3] Froomkin suggested that the disaster might have been avoided if journalists had access to the inspector's notes earlier.

Around early 2006, a military advocacy group called Soldiers for the Truth learned about a classified Pentagon report concerning body armor worn by U.S. soldiers fighting in Iraq. The group posted findings from the study on its Web site, prompting an investigation by reporter Michael Moss of the *New York Times.* "A secret Pentagon study has found that as many as 80 percent of the marines who have been killed in Iraq from wounds to the upper body could have survived if they had had extra body armor," Moss wrote. "Such armor has been available since 2003, but until recently the Pentagon has largely declined to supply it to troops despite calls from the field for additional protection, according to military officials."[4] In response to the article, the Senate and House Armed Services committees announced plans to hold hearings about the military's body armor program, and the U.S. Army awarded an emergency contract to upgrade soldiers' body armor. Why did the Pentagon keep its report a secret when the defective armor needed to be fixed as soon as possible?

Nobody can deny that the government must harbor *some* secrets to protect national security and maintain international relations. The problem is that the government has abused its power to withhold other information from the public.

Too much information is needlessly classified.

Classification of information as secret accelerated after the September 11 terrorist attacks. According to the government's Information Security Oversight Office, classification activities

Views on Government Secrecy

A number of legal scholars and politicians have voiced concerns about the seemingly all-encompassing way in which the U.S. government keeps information secret. Lawyer Ronald Goldfarb wrote: "Few would deny the justification for classifying some selective government information, but recent history has demonstrated that the process is far too extensive and has been abused."[*]

He found a similar opinion voiced by Thomas H. Kean, a former Republican governor of New Jersey, who chaired the commission that investigated the 9/11 attacks: "You'd just be amazed at the kind of information that's classified—everyday information, things we all know from the newspaper. We're better off with openness. The best ally we have in protecting ourselves against terrorism is an informed public."[**] A generation earlier, Senator Harold E. Hughes of Iowa wrote:

> Executive privilege is a license to kill—not people, but information, investigations, and ultimately the truth. This committee exposed the logical absurdity of the present administration's position when it obtained the shocking admission from the now-resigned Attorney General that executive privilege could be extended to every Federal employee.
>
> Unlimited use of executive privilege is the first step toward no holds-barred government.[***]

[*] Ronald Goldfarb, *In Confidence* (Ann Arbor, Mich.: Sheridan Books, 2009), p. 47.

[**] Scott Shane, "Since 2001, Sharp Increase in the Number of Documents Classified by the Government," *New York Times*, July 3, 2005.

[***] *Executive Privilege: Secrecy in Government, Freedom of Information, Hearings Before the Subcommittees on Intergovernmental Relations, Separation of Powers, and Administrative Practice and Procedure, Vol. 1* (Washington, D.C.: U.S. Government Printing Office, April–May 1973), p. 260.

during 2009 alone—eight years after the attacks—exceeded 54 million decisions.[5] These classification efforts can cost tax-payers more than $8 billion in a single year.[6] In recent years, many have criticized the federal government for classifying too much data. Yet overclassification is not new. In 2004, Representative Christopher Shays of Connecticut, chairman of the Subcommittee on National Security, Emerging Threats and International Relations, commented on the dilemma:

> This much we know: There are too many secrets. Soon after President Franklin Roosevelt's first executive order on classification in 1940, the propensity to overclassify was noted. Since then, a long and distinguished list of committees and commissions has studied the problem. They all found it impossible to quantify the extent of overclassification because no one even knows the full scope of the Federal Government's classified holding at any given time. Some estimate 10 percent of current secrets should never have been classified. Others put the extent of overclassification as high as 90 percent.[7]

What type of information is needlessly classified? J. William Leonard, who served as director of the Information Security Oversight Office, has said, "I've seen information that was classified that I've also seen published in third-grade text-books."[8] Examples of strange classifications include the Defense Intelligence Agency's deletion of a statement that former Chilean dictator Augusto Pinochet had an interest in fencing, boxing, and horseback riding; the Justice Department's removal of a four-line quotation of a *published* U.S. Supreme Court decision; and the classification of a plot against Santa Claus. Shays described a "For Official Use Only" report from the Department of Homeland Security Inspector General that reviewed the screening of trucks transporting urban solid waste from Canada into the United States. "So our conclusion," said Shays, "is

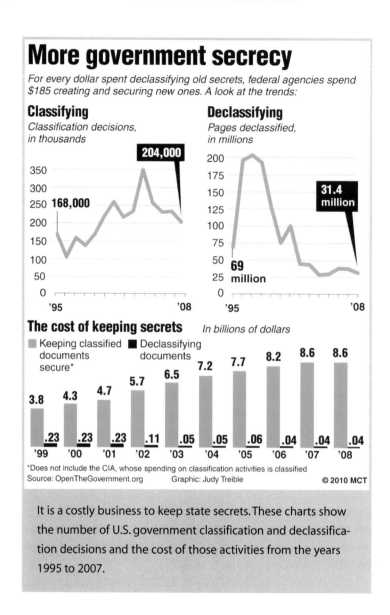

More government secrecy

For every dollar spent declassifying old secrets, federal agencies spend $185 creating and securing new ones. A look at the trends:

Classifying

Classification decisions, in thousands

204,000
168,000

'95 '08

Declassifying

Pages declassified, in millions

31.4 million

69 million

'95 '08

The cost of keeping secrets *In billions of dollars*

■ Keeping classified documents secure*   ■ Declassifying documents

	'99	'00	'01	'02	'03	'04	'05	'06	'07	'08
Keeping classified	3.8	4.3	4.7	5.7	6.5	7.2	7.7	8.2	8.6	8.6
Declassifying	.23	.23	.23	.11	.05	.05	.06	.04	.04	.04

*Does not include the CIA, whose spending on classification activities is classified
Source: OpenTheGovernment.org   Graphic: Judy Treible   © 2010 MCT

It is a costly business to keep state secrets. These charts show the number of U.S. government classification and declassification decisions and the cost of those activities from the years 1995 to 2007.

apparently there is a great deal the public should never know about Canadian garbage. Can you believe it?"[9]

The shifting disclosure policy for the National Intelligence Program budget provides another example. In 2007 and 2008, the total budget was declassified, whereas the 2006 budget was deemed classified. "How can that be, when more recent information is freely disclosed?" Aftergood asked. "No sensible answer is forthcoming."[10]

The practice of retroactive classification adds to the problem. For instance, the Defense Department released a report describing weaknesses in the National Missile Defense program and offering recommendations for testing the system. Shays posted the report on the Internet and journalists commented on the information in editorials and news articles. More than two years later, the Defense Department reclassified the recommendations. "Since the recommendations had already been released and publicized," said authors of a report prepared for Congress, "the retroactive classification did nothing to protect national security and served only to limit public debate on a controversial weapons system."[11]

Excessive secrecy even plagues officials within the federal government. In 2003, the Office of the Vice President denied a request by National Security Agency lawyers to see a copy of the Justice Department's legal analysis of the NSA's own terrorist surveillance program. "I cannot recall a more blatant example of using classification not for its intended purpose of denying information to our nation's adversaries but rather to use it as a bureaucratic weapon to blunt potential opposition," Leonard said. "To treat NSA lawyers who have the highest of clearance levels as if they were legal counsel for Al-Qaeda gives yet more fodder to our nation's adversaries to represent us as having contempt for the rule of law."[12]

Excessive classification jeopardizes national security.

Shays asserts that the culture of secrecy must end. "Against a rising tide of global terrorism," he said, "we are drowning in a sea of our own faux secrets, hiding public information from its real owners, the public, behind spurious ['For Official Use Only'] and ['Official Use Only'] labels. To right the balance between the public's right to know and countervailing public interest in security and privacy, the habits of secrecy must give way to the culture of shared information."[13] Increased information access does not only serve the ideal of democracy, Shays says; it is necessary for national security. The government devised classification practices during the Cold War, a struggle against the monolithic Soviet Union. Today, the United States struggles against terrorists, who are not associated with one nation. "Unreformed habits of secrecy blind us to the dispersed shards of information that, if linked, could reveal the enemy's shadowy plans," Shays warns.[14]

The 9/11 Commission, which investigated events leading to the terrorist attacks in 2001, concluded that a failure to share information may have been the most important reason why the U.S. government failed to prevent the plot. "There were bits and pieces of critical information available in different parts of the Government, in the CIA, the FBI, and the NSA," explained Richard Ben-Veniste of the National Commission on Terrorist Attacks upon the United States. "Some of the bits were bigger than others. But pieces of the information were never shared and never put together in time to understand the September 11 plot."[15]

A joint panel of the Senate and House intelligence committees also decided that information should have been shared with the public:

> Prior to September 11, the Intelligence Community and the U.S. Government labored to prevent attacks by Usama Bin Ladin and his terrorist network against the United States, but largely without the benefit of an alert, mobilized and committed American public. Despite intelligence information on the immediacy of the threat level in the spring and summer of 2001, the assumption prevailed in the U.S. Government that

attacks of the magnitude of September 11 could not happen here. As a result, there was insufficient effort to alert the American public to the reality and gravity of the threat.[16]

The U.S. Supreme Court case *Central Intelligence Agency v. Sims* (1985) taught that courts should defer to the CIA when the agency has decided that certain information must be withheld from the public. Some legal commentators suggest that the *Sims* decision has produced unintended effects:

> The sweeping secrecy that the *Sims* Court has sanctioned effectively blocks public and press efforts to evaluate CIA performance, thus making accountability difficult, if not impossible. Indeed, the CIA's widely publicized failures in connection with the 9/11 terrorist attacks illustrate the folly of unchecked secrecy, which not only cloaks questionable Agency activities but also conceals grave problems in CIA management. These problems were further evidenced in the CIA's miscalculations and false assessments of Iraqi weapons strength, which were used to justify the American invasion of Iraq. (Footnote omitted.)[17]

Following the investigation into the 9/11 terrorist attacks, Congress passed the Intelligence Reform and Terrorism Prevention Act of 2004. One of the aims of the law is to promote information sharing.

Exposing state secrets unmasks government misconduct.

To gain a political advantage, a federal agency may classify certain information as a secret. In *United States v. Reynolds* (1953), the case in which the U.S. Supreme Court bestowed its blessing to the state secrets privilege, the widows of the deceased civilians who died aboard a B-29 military aircraft wanted copies of the Air Force's accident-investigation report and statements from crash survivors. The Air Force asserted the state secrets privilege. The government filed affidavits claiming that disclosure of the information would seriously hamper national security and the development of highly technical and secret military equipment. Without reviewing the disputed reports, the Court agreed with the Air Force's refusal.

In February 2000, Judith Loether, daughter of one of the civilian observers who had died on the flight, found a copy of the declassified accident report posted on the Internet:

Criticism of the Critical Infrastructure Information (CII) Act

The CII Act of 2002 established a broad exemption to protect information from being released via the Freedom of Information Act and open-record laws of state and local governments. The purpose of the CII Act was to encourage the private sector to share information about critical infrastructure vulnerabilities with the Homeland Security Department, so that government analysts could devise ways to protect critical infrastructure and improve recovery measures in the event of a disaster.

The CII Act incited much disapproval. Senator Patrick Leahy of Vermont suggested that companies could use the exemption to shield themselves from liability for violating laws intended to protect U.S. citizens:

This bill goes far beyond what is needed to achieve the laudable goal of encouraging private sector companies to help protect our critical infrastructure. Instead, it will tie the hands of the federal regulators and law enforcement agencies working to protect the public from imminent threats. It will give a windfall to companies who fail to follow Federal health and safety standards. Most disappointingly, it will undermine the goals of openness in government that the FOIA was designed to achieve....

When I read this report, it was truly a sad, very dark comedy of errors that led to the terrible death of my father and eight other men. For instance, Engine No. 1 had caught on fire and it's reported by the co-pilot, who was a survivor, that the pilot actually turned off Engine No. 4 instead of Engine No. 1. The co-pilot saw this and thought he had corrected it, but they found later that he hadn't so both Engine No. 1 and Engine No. 4 had been turned off. They also discovered that Engine No. 2 had had a big loss of power and they think that the engineer, instead of cutting the fuel to the burning engine, had cut the fuel to Engine No. 2. So now you have the

In the end, the broad secrecy protections provided to critical infrastructure information in this bill will promote more secrecy which may undermine rather than foster national security. In addition, the immunity provisions in the bill will frustrate enforcement of the laws that protect the public's health and safety.[*]

One bizarre use of the CII exemption occurred in 2005. A New Jersey resident requested access to a township's electronic map of land parcels. The municipal utility denied access, because the utility had submitted the information to the Department of Homeland Security under the CII program. The New Jersey resident had another option, according to OMB Watch, a nonprofit research and advocacy organization. "[W]hile the municipal utility refuses to grant the resident free access to the database," OMB Watch reported, "they publicly offer paper copies of the maps for $5 apiece, leading some to speculate that the utility submitted the information to DHS specifically to avoid releasing the data *for free*."[**]

[*] "Homeland Security Act of 2002," *Congressional Record* 148 (November 19, 2002): S11425.
[**] "First Public Case of Critical Infrastructure Information," OMB Watch Web site, August 8, 2005. http://www.ombwatch.org/node/2557.

biggest bomber in the world with four propeller engines with now only one engine working. This was only part of all the things that went wrong that day.[18]

What about the report's disclosure of secret equipment? In 2003, the living heirs of the civilian observers filed a petition in the Supreme Court to reconsider the case. They addressed the government affidavits. "[I]t turns out that the Air Force's affidavits were false," the petitioners stated. "The Air Force recently declassified the accident reports. They include nothing approaching a 'military secret.' Indeed, they are no more than accounts of a flight that, due to the Air Force's negligence, went tragically awry. In telling the Court otherwise, the Air Force lied."[19]

Aftergood has proposed a category of government secrets called political secrecy. "It exploits the generally accepted legitimacy of genuine national security interests in order to advance a self-serving agenda, to evade controversy, or to thwart accountability," he said. "In extreme cases, political secrecy conceals violations of law and threatens the integrity of the political process itself."[20] Aftergood illustrates political secrecy with several examples. One can be found in a 1947 memo with the subject "Medical Experiments on Humans," which had been issued by the U.S. Atomic Energy Commission. "It is desired that no document be released which refers to experiments with humans and might have adverse effect on public opinion or result in legal suits," the memo advised. "Documents covering such work field should be classified 'secret.' "[21]

Aftergood also points to instances of political secrecy that occurred 60 years later: "[T]he Bush Administration secretly conducted domestic surveillance outside the statutory framework and performed interrogations subjecting suspected enemy combatants to extreme mental and physical pain."[22] Sometimes, the public must pierce the state secret veil to protect civil liberties.

Summary

The federal government's culture of secrecy, built up over generations, threatens the American public. Data classification hides information that could save lives. The practice of overclassification has veered so far out of control that up to 90 percent of classified data may be needlessly labeled as "secret." Overclassification hinders law enforcement agencies and prevents the American

QUOTABLE

Congress Tries to Rein in the State Secrets Privilege

In January 2008, Senator Edward M. Kennedy of Massachusetts sponsored the State Secrets Protection Act. The bill, which did not become law, would have limited the use of the state secrets privilege by the federal government. Kennedy discussed the *Reynolds* case and what he considered recent misuses of the privilege:

> In recent years, Federal courts have applied the *Reynolds* precedent to dismiss numerous cases—on issues ranging from torture, to extraordinary rendition, to warrantless wiretapping—without ever reviewing the evidence. Some courts have even upheld the executive's claims of state secrets when the purported secrets were publicly available, as in the case of *El-Masri v. Tenet*. In that case, there was extensive evidence in the public record that the plaintiff was kidnapped and tortured by the CIA on the basis of mistaken identity, but the court simply accepted at face value the Government's claim that litigation would require disclosure of state secrets. The court dismissed Mr. El-Masri's case without even evaluating the evidence or considering whether the case could be litigated on other evidence.
>
> When Federal courts accept the executive branch's state secrets claims as absolute, our system of checks and balances breaks down. By refusing to consider key pieces of evidence, or by dismissing lawsuits outright without considering any evidence at all, courts give the executive branch the ability to violate American laws and constitutional rights without any accountability or oversight, and innocent victims are left unable to obtain justice.

Source: "State Secrets Protection Act," *Congressional Record* 154 (January 23, 2008): S199.

public from protecting itself. Another aspect of the culture of secrecy is the overuse of the state secrets privilege. Government agencies have used the privilege to conceal civil liberty violations. "Governments are inclined too often to use constitutional and national-security claims to justify overclassifying information or intragovernmental communications as secret," Goldfarb said. "History has demonstrated too often how corrosive government in the dark can be."[23] Open-government laws provide a means to drag information concealed as state secrets into the light.

Targeted Transparency Effectively Promotes Freedom of Information

For more than a century, the federal government has used a mechanism other than the Freedom of Information Act and other open-records laws to promote freedom of information: targeted transparency. Targeted transparency laws promote a different type of freedom of information. Open-records laws, such as FOIA, compel government agencies to disclose certain information that reveals the inner workings of the government. In contrast, targeted transparency laws compel certain businesses and other organizations to disclose information to the public or to government agencies, which then release the information to the public. Although a targeted transparency law increases the flow of information to the public, its ultimate goal is to reduce risks to the public and improve products and services.

One of the earliest transparency efforts resulted from reports about unsanitary conditions in meatpacking plants and claims that contaminated food products caused deaths. Congress enacted the Pure Food and Drug Act of 1906, which required food manufacturers to label ingredients included in their products truthfully. Following the stock market crash of 1929, congressional hearings uncovered a variety of practices that companies concealed from the public, such as reporting exaggerated earnings. Under new laws, companies that offered stock to the public had to disclose accurate accounts of their businesses so that informed stock purchasers could assess true risks. More recently, targeted transparency rules have provided the public with a variety of valuable information. Individuals have used the information to improve the environment, provoke companies to manufacture safer cars, and encourage restaurant owners to improve hygiene.

Targeted disclosures improve the environment and the workplace.

On the night of December 2, 1984, the people of Bhopal, India, suffered a massive industrial accident. A storage tank inside a Union Carbide factory discharged 40 tons of methyl isocyanate gas, which spread through the city. Thousands of people inhaled the poison in their sleep and died. The disaster also impaired the health of more than 500,000 survivors.

In the wake of the Bhopal tragedy, Congress developed programs to enable U.S communities and their state governments to identify chemical dangers and devise disaster-relief procedures in the event of a toxin leak. For instance, the 1986 Emergency Planning and Community Right-to-Know Act requires manufacturing companies to inform the U.S. Environmental Protection Agency (EPA) about the amounts of toxic chemicals the companies release into the environment. The EPA publishes the submitted data as the Toxics Release Inventory.

Congress drafted the program to inform state and local governments, emergency responders, and the general public about toxic hazards in communities. As authors Archon Fung and Dara O'Rourke explain, many others employ Toxics Release Inventory data to compel polluters to change their ways:

> [The Toxics Release Inventory] has been used for purposes far beyond those imagined by its legislative authors. TRI data are now used regularly by individuals, community-based organizations, environmental

Dodging FOIA Requests

During the administration of President George W. Bush, Citizens Action New Mexico filed a FOIA request, seeking information about possible groundwater contamination. The group claimed that the New Mexico Environment Department had mismanaged the monitoring of wells at Sandia National Laboratory's Mixed Waste Landfill and that radioactive and hazardous chemicals might be leaching from the landfill into groundwater. The environmental activist group did not know that federal officials had found a way to avoid the FOIA request.

"Officials of the Environmental Protection Agency intentionally stopped keeping records concerning potentially hazardous landfills in New Mexico in order to circumvent the disclosure requirements of the Freedom of Information Act," reported Steven Aftergood of the Federation of American Scientists. "They also marked unclassified records as 'confidential' in order to restrict their dissemination, a report from the EPA Inspector General found."[*]

According to one EPA official, the agency staff did not keep written records of phone calls and conversations related to doubts about the groundwater monitoring network around the Mixed Waste Landfill. In this way, the EPA did not have records that it could hand over in response to a FOIA request. The EPA Inspector General concluded that the regional office had violated EPA policy and federal law, because the agency must prepare and preserve records of its decisions.[**]

[*] Steven Aftergood. "EPA Said to Have Suppressed, Misclassified Records," *Secrecy News*, May 5, 2010. http://www.fas.org/blog/secrecy/2010/05/epa_ig.html.

[**] *WatchDog TipSheet*, "Bush EPA Suppressed NM Waste Records to Sidestep FOIA," May 19, 2010. http://www.sej.org/publications/watchdog-tipsheet/bush-epa-suppressed-nm-waste-records-sidestep-foia.

groups, industry managers, state and federal agencies, lawyers, investment advisors, and the media. Uses vary from educating and mobilizing affected communities to assisting corporate environmental planning, from supporting efforts to strengthen regulations to promoting voluntaristic environmental initiatives.[1]

Private organizations analyze Toxics Release Inventory data, identify the largest polluters of toxins, and publish their findings. Faced with this publicity, large companies revise their manufacturing processes to decrease toxic emissions. Today, the Toxics Release Inventory covers the discharge of about 650 chemicals to the air, water, and land. According to the EPA, from 1988 to 2006, U.S. companies *decreased* releases of listed chemicals by 59 percent, which amounts to a drop of 1.77 billion pounds.[2]

The Occupational Safety and Health Administration requires a company to develop or obtain a Material Safety Data Sheet (MSDS) for each hazardous chemical that the company produces or imports. An MSDS includes information about signs and symptoms of exposure to the hazardous chemical, recommended exposure limits, physical characteristics of the hazardous chemical, and other data. Employers must ensure that MSDSs are readily available to their employees. The Emergency Planning and Community Right-to-Know Act requires companies that store certain amounts of hazardous chemicals to supply information about their MSDSs to the state emergency response commission, the local emergency planning committee, and the local fire department. The public can request copies of MSDSs from their local emergency planning committee.

Targeted disclosures also improve auto safety.

In 2000, the *New York Times* published a series of articles about traffic deaths associated with rollovers of sport utility vehicles. "The annual number of deaths involving rollovers has been inching up since 1993 as sport utility vehicles have become more popular," reported Keith Bradsher, who drew upon analyses of fatal car crashes in the United States. "Rollovers were a factor in 10,657 of the 35,806 deaths that occurred in vehicles of all types last year."[3] The problem spurred Congress to action. The Transportation Recall Enhancement, Accountability, and Documentation (TREAD) Act of 2000 requires government tests of each new model car and sport utility vehicle to measure crashworthiness and a tendency to rollover. The National Highway Traffic Safety Administration (NHTSA) rates vehicles based upon the test results, and the agency discloses ratings to the public in a brochure. The NHTSA also sponsors a Web site, SaferCar.gov, that provides safety-test results, tire ratings, known defects, defect investigations, and other useful information.

The TREAD Act further requires carmakers to report information about consumer complaints to the NHTSA. In the past, the NHTSA decided to open an investigation about a possible defect based on consumer complaints filed with the agency. "Our efforts to identify potential defects in a timely manner have been hampered by an inability to obtain relevant information in the possession of the manufacturers," explained Jeffrey W. Runge, who served as NHTSA's administrator. "Experience has shown that manufacturers often obtain information suggesting the existence of a safety-related problem months, and sometimes years, before consumer complaints to NHTSA indicate a potential problem."[4]

In short, the TREAD Act created a system in which a government agency collects information from car manufacturers and generates its own data about vehicle safety. The agency discloses much of this information to the public. By informing the public, Congress helps consumers to choose safer vehicles, which in turn motivates car manufacturers to improve their products. A 2005 report prepared for Congress stated that the average rating of tested vehicles had increased since the program started. "The improved ratings indicate that manufacturers have taken NCAP [New Car Assessment Program] seriously and designed and built vehicles that do well on NCAP tests," government researchers stated. "Automakers told us that vehicle safety and NCAP test results have become an important marketing tool. As a result, many auto manufacturers advertise five-star ratings in government crash tests in their television, radio, and print ads."[5]

Targeted disclosures improve health.

In the early twentieth century, newspapers reported on contaminated food products and the presence of questionable additives in foods, such as coal tar and borax. Congress decided to do something about the condition of the food industry. The Pure Food and Drug Act of 1906 forbade misbranding of foods with the objective of compelling companies to manufacture safe and wholesome products.

Labels that listed the ingredients of a food product helped to ensure that the product did not contain unwanted additives. Still, consumers had to wonder about the value of those listed ingredients. Just what did they mean? The Nutrition Labeling and Education Act of 1990 required food producers to add useful information to their labels: For each serving size, a label disclosed the amount of calories, fat, sodium, sugars, protein, dietary fiber, and other ingredients. With this information, consumers could evaluate the healthfulness of a packaged food and choose foods for an improved diet. Consumers' choices, enlightened by nutritional labeling, motivated manufacturers to design and produce more healthful food products.

What about the quality of food served in restaurants? The Centers for Disease Control and Prevention (CDC) estimates that about 76 million food-borne illnesses occur every year in the United States, resulting in the hospitalization of more than 300,000 people and the deaths of 5,000.[6] One CDC study suggests that about 52 percent of food-borne illness outbreaks may be associated with restaurants or delicatessens.[7] Following a series of news reports in 1997 about apparently common unsanitary practices in Los Angeles County restaurants, the

L.A. County Board of Supervisors initiated a targeted transparency program. The L.A. County Department of Health Services imposed a restaurant-hygiene letter grade based on

A New Transparency Policy Shines Light on Drug Regulation

During the Obama administration, the Food and Drug Administration set up a Transparency Task Force to find ways to reveal more information about agency decisions in an easy-to-use format and in a timely manner. Gardiner Harris of the *New York Times* explained that "the goal is to open up a system in which the agency failed to inform the public that a widely prescribed heartburn drug was especially toxic to babies; that a diabetes medicine and a painkiller increased heart attack risks; and that antidepressants increased suicidal thoughts and behavior in children and teenagers."[*] In the past, the FDA had withheld much information that pharmaceutical companies consider trade secrets or otherwise confidential.

In 2009 and 2010, the FDA task force sought public opinion on the best ways to make the information on agency activities and decision making more transparent, useful, and understandable to the public. For Phase I of the project, the agency launched "FDA Basics." The Web site offers webinars in which senior FDA officials answer questions from the public about the agency and the products it regulates, recorded conversations with FDA staff about their responsibilities, and videos that further explain the functions of FDA departments. During the next phase, the FDA disclosed proposals for additional types of disclosures that would help consumers. The task force requested comments on the proposals at public meetings and via a blog. "This initiative will make information about the FDA more user-friendly and accessible to the public," said FDA Commissioner Dr. Margaret A. Hamburg. "It fosters a better understanding about what we do."[**]

[*] Gardiner Harris, "Drug Agency May Reveal More Data on Actions," *New York Times*, June 2, 2009.

[**] U.S. Food and Drug Administration Web site, *FDA Unveils First Phase of Transparency Initiative*, January 12, 2010. http://www.fda.gov/NewsEvents/Newsroom/PressAnnouncements/ucm197222.htm.

inspections. Restaurant owners must post their letter grade in view of customers.

The hygiene-grading program enables consumers to avoid restaurants with poor hygiene practices. Over the years, restaurants that earned an A grade have enjoyed an increase in revenue; a

Health Information Flows Freely Through the Internet

For more than 150 years, countries have collaborated to detect and contain infectious diseases. Today, the World Health Organization (WHO) leads the coordination of data on infectious-disease surveillance. Yet a system of government reporting broke down in 2002 during the outbreak of severe acute respiratory syndrome (SARS), an infectious disease that first appeared in China and spread to 30 countries in six months. The earliest reports about the outbreak originated not from the Chinese government, but from Internet messages, cell phone calls, and ProMED-mail, a privately supported global electronic system for reporting outbreaks of infectious diseases. The Global Public Health Intelligence Network, an Internet-based early warning system that monitors global news wires and Web sites and that is part of the Public Health Agency of Canada, also detected SARS before the WHO. These reports compelled the WHO to ask the Chinese government about the problem. After the Chinese government acknowledged the outbreak, the WHO issued a global alert and warnings about travel.

The SARS incident showed that even though news about an epidemic became lost as it moved through governmental departments—a problem not unique to China—information still flowed from individuals to the WHO. In turn, the WHO and other health organizations, such as the CDC, provided the general public information about SARS through its Web sites and news releases.

Sources:

Stacey Knobler, Adel Mahmoud, Stanley Lemon, Alison Mack, Laura Sivitz, and Katherine Oberholtzer, eds., *Learning from SARS: Preparing for the Next Disease Outbreak* (Washington, D.C.: National Academies Press, 2004).

David A. Relman, Eileen R. Choffnes, and Alison Mack, eds., *Infectious Disease Movement in a Borderless World: Workshop Summary* (Washington, D.C.: National Academies Press, 2010).

B grade has brought a much smaller revenue increase, while C-grade establishments have experienced a revenue decline. Pressured to improve hygiene, an increasing number of restaurants have earned A grades. One study suggests that food-borne hospitalizations decreased following the introduction of the letter grade system.

In 2010, the New York City Board of Health adopted a similar letter-grade program for the city's restaurants, a number exceeding 24,000 establishments. "Giving consumers more information will help make our restaurants safer and cleaner," said New York City Health Commissioner Dr. Thomas A. Farley. "The grade in the window will give you a sense of how clean the kitchen is—and it will give every restaurant operator an incentive to maintain safe, sanitary conditions."[8]

Summary

Targeted transparency policies require government agencies, as well as private organizations, to divulge certain information to the pubic. These policies offer more than information disclosure. Whereas information release is an end point of freedom of information laws, targeted transparency laws attempt to reduce certain risks or improve products and services. That is, targeted transparency advances a defined public purpose, a goal achieved through a sequence of events: Information users perceive and understand newly disclosed information and therefore choose safer, healthier, or better-quality goods and services; information disclosers perceive and understand users' changed choices and therefore improve practices or products that in turn reduce risks or improve services.[9] Targeted transparency laws have been proven to reduce toxins in the environment and provide consumers with safer motor vehicles and more wholesome foods.

Targeted
Transparency Laws
Are Flawed

O n November 1, 2000, President Bill Clinton signed into law
the Transportation Recall Enhancement, Accountability, and
Documentation Act. With this new authority, Clinton remarked,

> comes the important responsibility to notify the pub-
> lic, as quickly as possible, of any relevant investigative
> efforts and other safety-related information submitted
> to the Secretary by the manufacturers or their suppli-
> ers. Thus, today I am also directing the Secretary of
> Transportation to implement the information disclo-
> sure requirements of the Act in a manner that assures
> maximum public availability of information.[1]

An example of targeted transparency, the TREAD Act
ensures public disclosure of government safety-test results

for new models of cars and sport utility vehicles, tire ratings, known defects, and investigations into defects by the National Highway Traffic Safety Administration. The TREAD Act also requires vehicle and tire manufacturers to report warranty and consumer complaint data—"early warning data"—to the NHTSA, which allows the agency to decide whether to investigate a possible defect. The NHTSA treats early-warning data as confidential.

In response to the NHTSA's policy about the confidentiality of early-warning data, the consumer group Public Citizen filed a lawsuit, arguing that the NHTSA should disclose the information to the public. In 2008, the U.S. Circuit Court of Appeals for the District of Columbia decided that the TREAD Act does not prevent disclosure of early-warning data. Public Citizen attorney Scott Nelson said he anticipated that the court's decision would lead to the availability of early-warning data in the near future. Apparently, the NHTSA would not reveal early-warning data on its Web site. Rather, individuals would be able to access the information by filing a Freedom of Information Act request.

The case shows that such a generally successful targeted transparency program has a fatal flaw: Individuals still must file a FOIA request to obtain data about vehicle safety. Although such targeted transparency efforts do generate detailed disclosures for the public, the disclosed information may not be useful and may even delude the public.

Disclosures can be misleading.

In March and April 1993, a microscopic parasite called cryptosporidium infested the water supply of Milwaukee, Wisconsin. Within weeks, more than 400,000 people became ill; many died.[2] Two years later, Senator Barbara Boxer of California urged the U.S. Senate to pass the Safe Drinking Water Act Amendments, which would require that customers must be informed about the purity of their drinking water:

Currently, consumers are required to be notified only if a water supplier violates an enforceable standard. Consumers do not have to be told if their tap water contains common contaminants which are not regulated, such as cryptosporidium and radioactive radon. We know cryptosporidium kills people. We do not happen to have a standard established for cryptosporidium. Does that mean we should not let people know if it is in their water supply?[3]

The Safe Drinking Water Act Amendments require each owner or operator of a public water system to notify consumers about the quality of their tap water. This law, however,

Missing Disclosures

Mesothelioma is a form of cancer that can line the lungs, heart, and other organs. Typically, mesothelioma develops because a person has previously inhaled asbestos particles; it may also signal that a victim will develop other disabling or lethal illnesses caused by asbestos. A 1977 rule of the Mine Safety and Health Administration requires companies to report work-related illnesses. The agency passes along the information to the public. Unfortunately, MSHA's rule has a flaw: The regulation applies only to illnesses suffered by active workers. Mesothelioma can develop 20 years or more *after* exposure to asbestos, a time when many workers have retired. Records obtained under the Freedom of Information Act revealed that one company did not report a trend of asbestos-related illnesses, such as mesothelioma, among retirees who had worked in its Minnesota mines. As a result, neither MSHA nor public pressure could urge safety improvements for mine employees.

In the mesothelioma case, a loophole in MSHA regulations led to the loss of disclosure. National security interests can also block the flow of information.

In December 2008, the earthen retaining wall of an ash pond collapsed at the Kingston Fossil Plant in eastern Tennessee, releasing a billion gallons of coal ash. A byproduct of burning coal for fuel, coal ash can contain mercury, arsenic, lead, provides an example of targeted transparency that has failed many people. In 2003, the Natural Resources Defense Council (NRDC), an environmental action group, published the results of an investigation into water-purity disclosures issued by 19 of America's largest cities. For many cities, the annual right-to-know reports did not warn the public about dangers lurking in their tap water. The NRDC found three causes of this failure:

- Right-to-know reports contained false or misleading statements. For instance, the cover pages of the 1999, 2000, and 2001 right-to-know reports for Washington, D.C., touted "Your Drinking Water Is Safe!" Yet the city's water had the highest levels of cyanide investigated in the NRDC study.

and other toxic compounds that can inflict heath problems in humans, such as birth defects and cancer. The toxic substances can also kill wildlife. Coal ash is stored throughout the United States at more than 1,300 sites. Typically, storage facilities are unmonitored and unregulated.

The public does not know the locations of coal ash storage sites. Earthjustice, the Sierra Club, and other environmental groups filed a FOIA request to discover the locations. The EPA released a list of 44 coal ash sites considered to have "high hazard potential," which means the agency decided that a failure of the facility would probably cause loss of human life. For now, the locations of the other thousand-plus coal ash sites remain secret. The Department of Homeland Security insists that coal ash is so toxic that terrorists may want to release the material into the environment.

Sources:

"Coal Ash Spills Too Dangerous to Reveal to Public, Says DHS," *Huffington Post*, June 12, 2009. http://www.huffingtonpost.com/2009/06/12/coal-ash-spills-too-dange_n_214739.html.

Shaila Dewan, "Hundreds of Coal Ash Dumps Lack Regulation," *New York Times*, January 7, 2009.

Greg Gordon, "On Range, Deadly Illness Went Unreported; Mesothelioma Strikes Years After Victims' Exposure to Asbestos," *Minneapolis Star Tribune*, August 21, 2005.

The group found that the drinking water also contained pollutants, such as bacteria and lead.

- Right-to-know reports omitted or buried information. As one example, a New Orleans report failed to include data on four contaminants found in drinking water. At least five other cities buried warnings about contaminants that may pose health risks to children and pregnant women, or that may promote the development of cancer. None of the surveyed cities reported known polluters of drinking water, as required by Environmental Protection Agency rules.

- Fewer than half of the surveyed cities offered reports translated into non-English languages used by many who lived in the community.

According to the NRDC, a defect in the Safe Drinking Water Act policy lies in the way that local governments have implemented the program. Another example of this type of failure can be found in food-label disclosures.

In early 2010, news outlets reported that certain packaged foods contain more calories than stated on their nutrition labels. Another investigation—performed by high school students using DNA analysis—revealed the mislabeling of foods. For example, investigators discovered that a cheese product was made from cow's milk, not sheep's milk as advertised. The U.S. Food and Drug Administration alerted food manufacturers that labeling on 22 products made unauthorized health claims and unauthorized nutrient content claims.

"For far too long, some of the world's biggest food manufacturers have designed their labels either to exaggerate the amount of healthy ingredients, or to imply that the food has magical, drug-like qualities that could prevent or treat various health problems," said Bruce Silverglade. "The Bush Administration gave manufacturers more and more license to deceive. But the party's over—or at least it should be."[4] Silverglade serves as the legal affairs director for the consumer advocacy group Center for Science in the Public Interest (CSPI). The group asserts that the FDA has not methodically tested the accuracy of food-package nutrition data for more than a decade. In its 2010 report "Food Labeling Chaos," CSPI revealed many examples of misleading food labels, such as:

- Orange juice labels with claims for protection of healthy joints due to the addition of glucosamine.
- Cereal labels with misinterpretations of scientific studies about the amount of sugar that may be consumed per day.
- Breakfast food claims that the presence of antioxidants helps support a person's immune system.
- Breakfast cereals with cancer-prevention claims.
- A boast for oatmeal that the inclusion of green tea promotes healthy arteries.
- A brand of English muffins that brags about the "goodness of whole grain," even though the main ingredient is white flour and the muffins contain more water than whole-wheat flour.
- Foods labeled "all natural" that contain foreign additives.

These false promises and statements may sell products but fail to inform the public as intended by the Nutrition Labeling and Education Act.

Disclosures can be too technical.

In 1983, the Occupational Safety and Health Administration (OSHA) sought to reduce illness and injuries from hazardous chemicals by disclosing information to employees. OSHA required chemical manufacturers and importers of chemicals to evaluate the hazard potential of the produced or imported chemicals, and disclose the results to businesses that purchase the chemicals. Under this regulation, employers must supply Material Safety Data Sheets to employees who work with hazardous materials. Armed with this information, employees theoretically could protect themselves from harm.

Twenty years later, OSHA discovered that while workers use MSDS data to explain the causes of their injuries and obtain better treatment, the chemical-hazard disclosure program has failed as a means for employees to *prevent* injuries. The information in MSDS disclosures is often presented in confusing technical language and terminology, a problem amplified for those workers with limited ability to read English. In addition, one survey indicated that the majority of MSDSs had inaccuracies in descriptions of health effects, appropriate first aid, and recommended protective measures. Targeted transparency experts Elena Fagotto and Archon Fung suggest that even readily understandable and accurate MSDSs probably would not ensure that workers could prevent injuries, because they would downplay the danger:

> Even if MSDSs were more user-friendly, individual psychological tendencies to misperceive and misunderstand risk would continue to hamper effective use of hazard information. According to Cass Sunstein of the University of Chicago, individuals are prone to probability neglect—that is, they tend to pay more attention to risks that involve extremely bad outcomes with remote probabilities, such as airplane crashes or tornadoes, while downplaying risks that are more probable but whose outcomes are not perceived as vividly, such as heart attacks or injuries from bicycle accidents.[5]

Disclosures can be too vague.

In March 2002, the federal government established the Homeland Security Advisory System, a now-defunct color-coded terrorism-threat warning program designed by the Department of Homeland Security (DHS). The scheme had five degrees of perceived danger: green indicated a low threat level; blue, a guarded level; yellow, an elevated threat level; orange, a high threat level; and red indicated a severe threat level. The system was set up to allow government agencies a chance to prevent, prepare for, and respond to a terrorist attack.

The threat alert system was also supposed to warn the public of an impending threat. During the first year of its use, DHS raised the threat level from yellow to orange four times without explaining the basis for heightened danger or advising citizens about how to protect themselves. Critics declared that the warnings were so vague that the public might question their authenticity. The warning system also produced feelings of helplessness, because a raised threat alert was often accompanied by advice to go about business as usual. At the time, psychologist Philip Zimbardo and author Bruce Kluger wrote:

> Forcing citizens to ride an emotional roller coaster without providing any clear instructions on how to soothe their jitters, the current security system has had a profoundly negative impact on our individual and collective mental health. I call this a "pre-traumatic stress syndrome," and its effect on our day-to-day lives is debilitating.[6]

Terrorism is about psychology, they argued, "about frightening ordinary people, making them feel confused and vulnerable. And, regrettably, the government is unwittingly engaging in this activity as effectively as Al Qaeda."[7]

Policy conflicts can block disclosure programs.

In 2000, the Institute of Medicine's Committee on Quality of Health Care in America published an overview of studies into medical mistakes committed in hospitals. One study suggested that at least 44,000 Americans die every year as a result of medical errors, whereas another study placed the number as high as 98,000.[8] The committee recommended a nationwide mandatory reporting system to collect and disclose medical errors that cause deaths or serious harm. The general public and organizations that purchase health care could use the information to select hospitals with good track records. These informed choices would pressure hospitals to improve the quality of health care.

In 2009, Consumers Union published its investigation into the progress of medical-error reporting. Conflicts arising from concerns about confidentiality and hospital liability thwarted efforts to launch a national, mandatory system for reporting and disclosing hospital errors. By October 2007, 25 states and the District of Columbia had set up systems for hospitals to report medical errors. The vast majority operate on the basis that data remain confidential. Meanwhile, preventable medical harm may account for at least 100,000 deaths each year.[9]

The 1986 Emergency Planning and Community Right-to-Know Act requires companies to notify the EPA about the amounts of toxic chemicals that they discharge into the environment. Although the EPA consistently discloses submitted data as the Toxics Release Inventory, the contents vary according to policy. The Clinton administration expanded disclosure by increasing the number of chemicals covered by the inventory. The administration also lowered the minimum amount of a hazardous chemical released that would trigger a reporting obligation. A company had to file a detailed report if it discharged 500 pounds or more of a listed chemical.

In December 2006, the Bush administration reduced the quantity and quality of chemical data submitted for the Toxics Release Inventory. Now, a company could file a shorter, less-detailed report if it used less than 5,000 pounds of toxic chemicals or released less than 2,000 pounds of toxic chemicals into the environment. The change allowed more than 3,500 facilities to decrease their reporting. Thirteen states sued the EPA over the relaxed policy, asserting that the change strangled public disclosure of information about chemical hazards. In 2009, the Obama administration reinstated higher thresholds for reporting and overturned the relaxed reporting regulations of the Bush administration.

Conflicts Between Public Disclosure and National Security

Amendments to the Clean Air Act of 1990 required 66,000 industrial facilities to supply the EPA with data on estimates of human casualties from accidents at sites where dangerous chemicals are stored, as well as emergency-response plans to deal with such disasters. The law gave companies until June 1999 to transfer information to the EPA, which would then disclose the data to the public. When the EPA announced a plan to offer submitted worst-case scenario information on the Internet, the FBI, the CIA, and the Defense and State departments objected, asserting that terrorists could easily access the information to find targets. Environmental groups argued that the risks posed by industrial accidents outweighed any increased risks of terrorist attacks.

Eventually, public interest groups dodged the debate by publishing information about chemical accident risks on the Internet: About 14,000 summaries of worst-case scenarios submitted to the EPA. Although these were executive summaries, not the full reports that the EPA had originally planned to post on its Web site, the information gave the public a sense of risks posed by various companies.

Despite continuing pressure from the U.S. intelligence community, public interest groups eventually succeeded in persuading the EPA to post worst-case scenario data on the Internet. Following the terrorist attacks of September 11, 2001, however, the agency removed the information from its Web site. Worst-case scenario information can still be found in federal reading rooms, many available to the public by appointment only.

Sources:
Carl Hulse, "Group Puts Disaster Data on Internet," *New York Times*, September 12, 1999.
Jillian Lloyd, "Terrorist Threat vs. Public Disclosure," *Christian Science Monitor*, December 9, 1998.

Summary

David Weil, co-director of the Transparency Policy Project at Harvard's Kennedy School of Government, asserts that, as a means to improve products and services, targeted transparency has failed:

> Most people support the general idea of transparency because, as noted, it is basic to democracy. However, targeted transparency gives rise to new questions. When does it work? What factors link disclosure to changes in behavior that achieve public objectives? After reviewing eighteen major transparency policies, our conclusion is that more often than not they do not work. They sometimes do not work because they are political compromises that were never intended to work. More often, they don't work because they haven't been designed terribly well, and the policymakers haven't really considered what they want to accomplish through transparency.[10]

The public also cannot rely upon targeted transparency policies to promote freedom of information. Conflicting interests may ensure that some transparency programs are never realized. Other transparency programs disclose information to the public, but may convey misleading or false statements, information presented in highly technical terms, or a disclosure can be so vague that it lacks useful information.

A Matter
of Balance

Americans value freedom of information as a concept. Yet implementing freedom of information to create an open government creates challenges. For example, advocates for an open government praised the Obama administration for reversing the trend of increased government secrecy. As soon as he took office, President Barack Obama signed an executive order and two memoranda that restored a presumption of openness when a federal agency responds to a Freedom of Information Act request and instructed agencies to improve transparency. Obama also set goals for declassifying documents while reducing new classification of records. Later that year, Attorney General Eric H. Holder Jr. issued a memorandum on policies to limit the use of the state secrets privilege to block disclosure of government documents. Holder said the Department of Justice would not defend an agency's claim of the privilege to conceal violations of law, inefficiency, or administrative error, or to prevent embarrassment to a U.S. government agency or organization. Under the policy, the government would raise the privilege in court only if disclosure threatened a genuine harm to national defense or foreign relations.

Within the first year, however, advocates of government transparency criticized the Obama administration. For example, the government set up a Web site, www.recovery.gov, to track the uses of the $787 billion economic recovery package. Commentators described the site as confusing and hard to navigate. Others wanted Obama to use the White House Web site to live-stream cabinet meetings and other high-level meetings.

A major controversy concerned efforts to disclose photographs of prisoner abuse at the Abu Ghraib prison in Iraq. After the ACLU requested photos of detainee abuse, two federal courts ordered the photos released. Although the White House announced an agreement with the Department of Defense to disclose the photos, within a month, Obama reversed the decision. Before the end of the year, the president signed the Department of Homeland Security Appropriations Act of 2010, which included a section called the Open FOIA Act of 2009. The ironically named Open FOIA Act forbids disclosure of photographs that relate "to the treatment of individuals engaged, captured, or detained after September 11, 2001, by the Armed Forces of the United States in operations outside of the United States."[1]

The government's ban on the release of the prison photos became one of the biggest disappointments for open-government advocates. The decision to withhold the photographs was not uninformed, however. Generals testified in Congress that disclosure of the photos could endanger the lives of U.S. soldiers. In other words, the generals asserted that privacy and national security interests trump a freedom of information policy.

Can An Open Government Co-exist with Personal Privacy Interests?

Establishing a transparent U.S. government would allow Americans to inspect agency functions and their decision-making processes. A part of those agency functions, however, involves private information about U.S. citizens collected and stored by local, state, and federal governments. A truly open government would enable the public to examine this private data, and that would conflict with the fundamental value of privacy. Some argue that such a widespread breach of privacy resulting from free access to government records would threaten the reputations, livelihoods, and even the lives of American citizens.

Others contend that an open government does not require allowing the public to access all information stored in government records. In any event, laws protect the privacy of individuals. The Freedom of Information Act itself establishes exemptions against invasions of privacy. Other federal laws—and the U.S. Constitution—also protect personal privacy. State constitutions, state laws, and common law complement privacy rights granted by the federal government.

Should the Need to Guard State Secrets Always Trump Government Transparency?

The U.S. government must maintain certain secrets to ensure national security and promote diplomatic relations. Government agencies protect state secrets by classifying records, and, if necessary, by asserting the state secrets privilege in court. The importance of protecting state secrets is illustrated by the deference that judges give to government agencies about such information, as well as by the first exemption of the Freedom of Information Act, which prevents disclosure of state secrets. The Supreme Court–approved mosaic theory, which protects apparently innocuous data that might reveal a state secret, further prevents freedom of information laws from exposing certain information.

Although commentators acknowledge the necessity of state secrets, some argue that the federal government's culture of secrecy threatens the American public. The practice of overclassification—to the point where up to 90 percent of classified data may be needlessly labeled as "secret"—hobbles law enforcement agencies and prevents the American public from protecting itself. Government agencies also use the state secrets privilege to conceal civil-liberties violations and errors of government employees. A legitimate need to guard some state secrets, the argument goes, must not automatically suppress freedom of information.

Are Targeted Transparency Laws Effective?

Targeted transparency laws require government agencies, as well as private organizations, to disclose certain information on a regular basis to the public. Targeted transparency policies achieve more than information disclosure: They reduce certain risks or

QUOTABLE

Steven Aftergood, director of the Federation of American Scientists Project on Government Secrecy

If all government secrecy actions were uniformly bad or abusive, the public policy solution would be simple: to eliminate secrecy. If all government secrecy actions were necessary or prudent, no solution would be required, since there would be no problem. But in practice, government secrecy seems to be comprised of a shifting mix of the legitimate and the illegitimate. Genuine national security secrecy is diluted in an ocean of unnecessary bureaucratic secrets and defamed from time to time by abuse in the form of political secrecy. The enduring public policy problem is to disentangle the legitimate from the illegitimate, preserving the former and exposing the latter.

Source: Steven Aftergood, "Reducing Government Secrecy: Finding What Works," *Yale Law & Policy Review* 27, No. 2 (Spring 2009), p. 404.

improve products and services. Targeted transparency accomplishes these goals by informing the public so that individuals can select safer, healthier, or better-quality goods and services. Companies improve their services and products to ensure a market for informed consumers.

Some experts argue that targeted transparency polices often fail as a method for informing the public and for improving goods and services. One problem lies with policymakers who did not carefully design a targeted transparency law with specific goals in mind. Even when the goals are clear, conflicting interests may strangle a targeted transparency law before it is put into action. Some transparency programs mature to the stage in which the government discloses information to the public. Yet the information may be flawed due to misleading or false statements, information offered in a form incomprehensible to the general public, or a disclosure can be too vague to serve a useful purpose.

Should the Public Be Able to Access Law Enforcement Records?

In the late 1970s, law enforcement officials complained that freedom of information laws had eroded the ability of law enforcement agencies to gather information. For example, citizens had withheld information from the FBI because they feared that an FOIA request of FBI records would expose their identities. Law enforcement officials also found difficulty in recruiting and maintaining informants. Today, FOIA Exemption 7 protects from disclosure information compiled for law enforcement purposes but only to the extent that disclosure:

- could reasonably be expected to interfere with enforcement proceedings;
- would deprive a person of the right to a fair trial;
- could reasonably be expected to constitute an unwarranted invasion of personal privacy;

- could reasonably be expected to disclose the identity of a confidential source, and information supplied by a confidential source;

- would disclose techniques and procedures for law enforcement investigations or prosecutions, if disclosure could reasonably be expected to allow a person to evade the law;

- could reasonably be expected to endanger the life or physical safety of any individual.

Professor James T. O'Reilly describes how the law enforcement exemption raises its own issues:

> [T]he law enforcement exemption has often stirred controversy. Police activity is the government's most controversial point of impact on the general public. A law intended to hold government more accountable to the public would naturally alarm government's law enforcement managers, for greater accountability would carry with it the dissemination of more information to the small segment of the public that commits crimes. And this exemption is the point of much conflict between advocates of greater accountability and advocates of stronger police work. (Footnote omitted.)[2]

Application of a freedom of information policy to law enforcement records continues to incite familiar conflicts: Freedom of information impedes the ability of government to perform a function—in this case, law enforcement—and freedom of information threatens personal privacy.

How Does Privatization Affect Open Government?

The term *privatization* refers to the transfer of a government responsibility to private control. Federal, state, and local governments hire businesses to carry out a service traditionally performed by the government, such as school bus transportation, running schools and hospitals, operating prisons, or performing military duties. As lawyer Craig D. Feiser explains, the Freedom of Information Act does not account for privatization:

> [N]either the President nor Congress could have realized, in 1966, the problems that would result once the Act was applied to the myriad of government operations. One of these problems, especially important since the 1980s, is whether to apply the Act to private entities. This issue is important because, as government agencies turn to private entities in order to function more efficiently, courts have had to deal with FOIA requests for information relating to the government but created or possessed by entities not explicitly covered under the Act. Debates therefore have developed regarding the benefits and drawbacks of privatization, including its effects on freedom of information.
>
> As privatization of government services continues ... some commentators worry that the desire for government efficiency will cause information that is important to the public to become shrouded in secrecy. (Footnotes omitted.)[3]

Like the FOIA, many other public-records laws apply to documents controlled by an "agency," which typically excludes government contractors. Since open-records laws usually do not mention private contractors, courts must interpret the laws. Many courts have devised complicated tests to determine whether a company is an agency for the purpose of an open-records law. Judges have applied the tricky tests inconsistently.

Government departments also hire contractors to manage and store government records. This practice throws up another barrier to public access, because a government agency no longer controls the documents. Instead, a private company possesses and controls the information.

Summary

Few would argue against the value of an open government. Freedom of information programs help to reveal the inner workings of government agencies and ensure that the government is held accountable. Yet government transparency can threaten personal privacy, because government agencies collect and store a wealth of personal information about U.S. citizens. Beth Givens, founder and director of the Privacy Rights Clearinghouse, emphasizes that "[o]ne of the most challenging public policy issues of our time is the balancing act between access to public records and personal privacy—the difficulty of accommodating

Shining Light on an Oil Spill

On April 20, 2010, an explosion erupted aboard the Deepwater Horizon, an oil platform in the Gulf of Mexico. According to government estimates, a damaged well spewed more than one million gallons of oil into the ocean each day, creating the largest oil spill in U.S. history—a massive, 300-foot thick plume extending three miles wide and 10 miles long. At first, most of the oil spill polluted coastlines in Louisiana. In June, oil had reached Alabama, Mississippi, and Florida. In every place the spill washed up, it killed wildlife and damaged fishing and tourism industries. A Coast Guard commander said that the effects of the immense oil spill could persist for years.

Congress immediately began an investigation of the disaster and interrogated executives of BP, the oil company that had leased and operated the Deepwater Horizon. Meanwhile, news reporters and advocacy groups, including Greenpeace and Citizens for Responsibility and Ethics in Washington, filed FOIA requests to obtain government inspection records. Documents indicated that the Minerals Management Service, a bureau in the U.S. Department of the Interior, had inspected the Deepwater Horizon less frequently than normal. Journalists also reported that, as early as 10 months before the explosion, BP had concerns about the stability of the well casing and the both personal privacy interests and the public interest of transparent government."[4]

An open-government policy also raises another conflict: The government must keep certain information secret in order to function, particularly in the area of national security. Again, competing interests require a balance between disclosure and concealment. "Balance is more difficult than a policy of unthinking secrecy or unthinking disclosure," said John Podesta, who served as President Clinton's White House chief of staff. "In pursuing a balanced approach, we . . . seek to protect national security but also to be true to our most fundamental values as

function of the blowout preventer, a fail-safe device that should have sliced through the drill pipe to shut off the well.

While FOIA requests offered clues to the origins of the disaster, the federal government provided information about recovery efforts. In June, the National Oceanic and Atmospheric Administration (NOAA) launched a federal Web site, www.geoplatform.gov/gulfresponse, to supply near-real-time information about the response to the oil spill. Integrating data from Homeland Security, NOAA, the Coast Guard, the Fish and Wildlife Service, the EPA, and other agencies, the Web site offered information on the oil spill's path, areas closed to fishing, status of wildlife, and resources deployed in the Gulf Coast.

Sources:

"Federal Agencies Introduce Online Mapping Tool to Track Gulf Response," Deepwater Horizon Response Web site, June 14, 2010. http://www.deepwaterhorizonresponse. com/go/doc/2931/656543.

"Gulf of Mexico Oil Spill (2010)," New York Times, June 17, 2010. http://topics.nytimes. com/top/reference/timestopics/subjects/o/oil_spills/gulf_of_mexico_2010/index. html?inline=nyt-classifier.

Michael Kunzelman and Garance Burke, "Deepwater Horizon Inspections: MMS Skipped Monthly Inspections on Doomed Rig," Huffington Post, May 17, 2010. http://www. huffingtonpost.com/2010/05/16/deepwater-horizon-inspect_n_578079.html.

Ian Urbina, "Documents Show Early Worries about Safety of Rig," New York Times, May 29, 2010.

a nation. For over two centuries, we have prospered and won because—at our best—we have found ways to do both."[5]

The Obama administration tried a new type of information disclosure. The Web site Data.gov offers data sets of government information previously unavailable to the public and allows the American people to find ways to use the data. After the first year of operation, Data.gov offered more than 250,000 data sets and hundreds of applications created by third parties, such as applications that enable individuals to check the safety and environmental health of a neighborhood, and applications that enable travelers to find the fastest route to their destinations. On Data.gov's first anniversary, U.S. Chief Information Officer Vivek Kundra challenged the public. "So all you innovators out there," he said, "what data sets can we try to get out there to help you go further?"[6]

Beginning Legal Research

The goals of each book in the POINT/COUNTERPOINT series are not only to give the reader a basic introduction to a controversial issue affecting society, but also to encourage the reader to explore the issue more fully. This Appendix is meant to serve as a guide to the reader in researching the current state of the law as well as exploring some of the public policy arguments as to why existing laws should be changed or new laws are needed.

Although some sources of law can be found primarily in law libraries, legal research has become much faster and more accessible with the advent of the Internet. This Appendix discusses some of the best starting points for free access to laws and court decisions, but surfing the Web will uncover endless additional sources of information. Before you can research the law, however, you must have a basic understanding of the American legal system.

The most important source of law in the United States is the Constitution. Originally enacted in 1787, the Constitution outlines the structure of our federal government, as well as setting limits on the types of laws that the federal government and state governments can enact. Through the centuries, a number of amendments have added to or changed the Constitution, most notably the first 10 amendments, which collectively are known as the "Bill of Rights" and which guarantee important civil liberties.

Reading the plain text of the Constitution provides little information. For example, the Constitution prohibits "unreasonable searches and seizures" by the police. To understand concepts in the Constitution, it is necessary to look to the decisions of the U.S. Supreme Court, which has the ultimate authority in interpreting the meaning of the Constitution. For example, the U.S. Supreme Court's 2001 decision in *Kyllo v. United States* held that scanning the outside of a person's house using a heat sensor to determine whether the person is growing marijuana is an unreasonable search—if it is done without first getting a search warrant from a judge. Each state also has its own constitution and a supreme court that is the ultimate authority on its meaning.

Also important are the written laws, or "statutes," passed by the U.S. Congress and the individual state legislatures. As with constitutional provisions, the U.S. Supreme Court and the state supreme courts are the ultimate authorities in interpreting the meaning of federal and state laws, respectively. However, the U.S. Supreme Court might find that a state law violates the U.S. Constitution, and a state supreme court might find that a state law violates either the state or U.S. Constitution.

Not every controversy reaches either the U.S. Supreme Court or the state supreme courts, however. Therefore, the decisions of other courts are also important. Trial courts hear evidence from both sides and make a decision, while appeals courts review the decisions made by trial courts. Sometimes rulings from appeals courts are appealed further to the U.S. Supreme Court or the state supreme courts.

Lawyers and courts refer to statutes and court decisions through a formal system of citations. Use of these citations reveals which court made the decision or which legislature passed the statute, and allows one to quickly locate the statute or court case online or in a law library. For example, the Supreme Court case *Brown v. Board of Education* has the legal citation 347 U.S. 483 (1954). At a law library, this 1954 decision can be found on page 483 of volume 347 of the U.S. Reports, which are the official collection of the Supreme Court's decisions. On the following page, you will find samples of all the major kinds of legal citation.

Finding sources of legal information on the Internet is relatively simple thanks to "portal" sites such as findlaw.com and lexisone.com, which allow the user to access a variety of constitutions, statutes, court opinions, law review articles, news articles, and other useful sources of information. For example, findlaw.com offers access to all Supreme Court decisions since 1893. Other useful sources of information include gpo.gov, which contains a complete copy of the U.S. Code, and thomas.loc.gov, which offers access to bills pending before Congress, as well as recently passed laws. Of course, the Internet changes every second of every day, so it is best to do some independent searching.

Of course, many people still do their research at law libraries, some of which are open to the public. For example, some state governments and universities offer the public access to their law collections. Law librarians can be of great assistance, as even experienced attorneys need help with legal research from time to time.

Common Citation Forms

Source of Law	Sample Citation	Notes
U.S. Supreme Court	*Employment Division v. Smith*, 485 U.S. 660 (1988)	The U.S. Reports is the official record of Supreme Court decisions. There is also an unofficial Supreme Court ("S. Ct.") reporter.
U.S. Court of Appeals	*United States v. Lambert*, 695 F.2d 536 (11th Cir.1983)	Appellate cases appear in the Federal Reporter, designated by "F." The 11th Circuit has jurisdiction in Alabama, Florida, and Georgia.
U.S. District Court	*Carillon Importers, Ltd. v. Frank Pesce Group, Inc.*, 913 F.Supp. 1559 (S.D.Fla.1996)	Federal trial-level decisions are reported in the Federal Supplement ("F. Supp."). Some states have multiple federal districts; this case originated in the Southern District of Florida.
U.S. Code	Thomas Jefferson Commemoration Commission Act, 36 U.S.C., §149 (2002)	Sometimes the popular names of legislation—names with which the public may be familiar—are included with the U.S. Code citation.
State Supreme Court	*Sterling v. Cupp*, 290 Ore. 611, 614, 625 P.2d 123, 126 (1981)	The Oregon Supreme Court decision is reported in both the state's reporter and the Pacific regional reporter.
State Statute	Pennsylvania Abortion Control Act of 1982, 18 Pa. Cons. Stat. 3203-3220 (1990)	States use many different citation formats for their statutes.

Statutes

Freedom of Information Act, Public Law 89-554 (5 U.S.C. §552)

Enacted in 1966, the Freedom of Information Act allows disclosure of information under the control of federal executive branch agencies.

Privacy Act of 1974, Public Law 93-579 (5 U.S.C. §552a)

The law requires federal agencies to ensure the security and confidentiality of records that contain personal data. The Privacy Act includes exceptions to allow a federal agency to release an individual's private information without the consent of that individual.

The 1986 Emergency Planning and Community Right-to-Know Act, Public Law 99-499 (42 U.S.C. §11001)

The law requires manufacturing companies to inform the EPA about the amounts of toxic chemicals that they release into the environment. The EPA publishes the submitted data as the Toxics Release Inventory.

The Electronic Communications Privacy Act of 1986, Public Law 99-508 (18 U.S.C. §2510)

Under this law, providers of electronic communications services, such as telephone companies and Internet service providers, must restrict access to the contents of stored computerized records. The act covers subscriber information, transaction records, and the content of communications.

The Nutrition Labeling and Education Act of 1990, Public Law 101-535 (21 U.S.C. §301)

The law requires food producers to add information to their labels about the contents of food products.

Electronic Freedom of Information Act Amendments of 1996, Public Law 104-231 (5 U.S.C. §552)

The law requires federal agencies to make information available electronically.

The Safe Drinking Water Act Amendments of 1996, Public Law 104-182 (42 U.S.C. §201)

The law requires each owner or operator of a public water system to notify consumers about the quality of their tap water.

The Transportation Recall Enhancement, Accountability, and Documentation Act of 2000, Public Law 106-414 (49 U.S.C. §30101)

The law requires government tests of each new model car and sport utility vehicle to measure crashworthiness and a tendency to roll over. The National Highway Traffic Safety Administration rates vehicles based upon the test results, and the agency discloses ratings to the public in printed form and on its Web site.

Critical Infrastructure Information Act of 2002, Public Law 107-296 (6 U.S.C. §101)

The CII Act established an exemption to protect information from the FOIA and open-records laws of state and local governments. The purpose of the CII Act was to encourage the private sector to share information about critical infrastructure vulnerabilities with the Department of Homeland Security, so that government analysts could devise ways to protect critical infrastructure and improve recovery measures in the event of a disaster.

Openness Promotes Effectiveness in Our National Government Act of 2007, Public Law 110-175 (5 U.S.C. §552a, et seq.)

Among other things, the OPEN Government Act recognized a new type of news media requester entitled to reduced fees: bloggers and writers who publish on Web sites.

Cases

United States v. Reynolds, 345 U.S. 1 (1953)

The Supreme Court held that, after the government asserts a claim of executive privilege, a court must decide whether the circumstances are appropriate for the claim of privilege without forcing the government to disclose the information. If a court decides that the government properly claimed the privilege, the court cannot compel disclosure of the information. The case established the strength of executive privilege, or state secrets privilege.

Griswold v. Connecticut, 381 U.S. 479 (1965)

The Supreme Court considered a Connecticut statute that made it a crime for any person to use any drug or article to prevent conception, or to offer advice on the use of contraceptives. The Court held that the law was unconstitutional because it violated a right to privacy. *Griswold* started a series of privacy cases that protects individual privacy rights from intrusion by federal and state governments.

EPA v. Mink, 410 U.S. 73 (1973)

When an agency refuses to comply with a FOIA request on the grounds that the requested information fell within the national security exemption, the Supreme Court ruled, a judge could only determine whether the agency had stamped the document as "classified," but could not review the document in private. A year later, Congress gave judges the authority to review classified documents to determine whether they had been properly classified.

Central Intelligence Agency v. Sims, 471 U.S. 159 (1985)

The Supreme Court agreed with the CIA's decision to protect the names of researchers who had served as intelligence sources, as well as the names of the researchers' institutions, which may be used to discover the identities of the researchers. Other courts have applied the *Sims* mosaic theory rationale to records held by various federal agencies.

U.S. Department of State v. Ray, 502 U.S. 164 (1991)

In a case involving Haitian refugees interviewed by the U.S. Department of State, the Supreme Court held that the government had lawfully removed identifying data under Exemption 6 of the FOIA to protect the privacy of the interviewees.

ACLU v. FBI, **429 F. Supp. 2d 179 (D.D.C. 2006)**
A federal judge ruled that the FBI had properly relied upon Exemption 1 of the FOIA to withhold documents about the agency's surveillance of certain U.S. political and religious organizations, because disclosure would reveal the names of intelligence sources and operational methods.

Azmy v. U.S. Department of Defense, **562 F.Supp. 2d 590 (S.D.N.Y. 2008)**
A federal judge ruled that the U.S. Department of Defense had properly invoked Exemption 1 of the FOIA to withhold documents that would expose intelligence methods used by government personnel to assemble and coordinate intelligence data, and plans for future intelligence gathering.

Terms and Concepts

Classification
Common law
Executive order
Executive privilege
Freedom of information
Freedom of Information Act
Government transparency
Mosaic theory
Open government
Presumption
Privacy Act
Privacy rights
Privatization
Right to know
State secrets
State secrets privilege
Statutory law
Targeted transparency

Introduction: The Necessary, but Controversial, Right

1 Scott Shane and Charlie Savage, "Documents Detail Conditions Found at Secret C.I.A. Jails," *New York Times*, November 1, 2009.

2 Ellen M. Katz, "Transparency in Government: How American Citizens Influence Public Policy," in Paul Malamud, ed., *Transparency in Government* (Washington, D.C.: U.S. State Department, n/d), http://usinfo.org/enus/government/overview/transgov.html.

3 Charles Francis Adams, *The Works of John Adams, Second President of the United States: With a Life of the Author, Notes and Illustrations, Vol. 3* (Boston: Charles C. Little and James Brown, 1851), p. 448.

4 Frank Moore, *American Eloquence: A Collection of Speeches and Addresses by the Most Eminent Orators of America, Vol. I* (New York: D. Appleton, 1859), p. 36.

5 "The Right to Know," *New York Times*, January 23, 1945.

6 Michael R. Lemov, "John Moss and the Battle for Freedom of Information, 41 Years Later," Nieman Watchdog Web site, July 3, 2007. http://www.niemanwatchdog.org/index.cfm?fuseaction=background.view&backgroundid=00191&stoplayout=true&print=true.

7 "U.S. Aide Defends Lying to Nation," *New York Times*, December 7, 1962.

8 Representative John E. Moss, speaking for the Freedom of Information Act, on June 20, 1966, to the House of Representatives, 89th Cong., 2nd sess., *Congressional Record* 112, p. 13642.

9 Bill Moyers, "Bill Moyers on the Freedom of Information Act," "NOW with Bill Moyers," April 5, 2002. http://www.pbs.org/now/printable/transcript_moyers4_print.html.

10 Martha Mendoza, "AP Review Finds Federal Government Missing Deadlines and Time Limits," Associated Press Web site, March 13, 2006. http://www.ap.org/FOI/foi_031306b.html.

11 President Barack Obama, memorandum of January 21, 2009, on the Freedom of Information Act, *Federal Register* 74, No. 15 (January 26, 2009), p. 4683.

12 "Managing the News," *New York Times*, October 31, 1962.

Point: An Open Government Infringes Privacy Rights

1 Eric Lichtblau, "Social Security Opened Its Files for 9/11 Inquiry," *New York Times*, June 22, 2005.

2 Frederick S. Lane, *American Privacy* (Boston: Beacon Press, 2009), p. 1.

3 *Wheaton v. Peters*, 33 U.S. 591, 634 (1834).

4 Samuel Warren and Louis D. Brandeis, "The Right to Privacy," *Harvard Law Review* 4, No. 5 (December 15, 1890), p. 205.

5 J. Holbrook, *Ten Years Among the Mail Bags* (New York: Loomis National Library Association, 1888), p. 6.

6 "Lament of a Census Taker," *Yarbrough Family Quarterly* 2 (1992), p. 10.

7 "Trials of the Census-Taker," *New York Times*, July 19, 1875.

8 Daniel J. Solove, "Access and Aggregation: Public Records, Privacy and the Constitution," *Minnesota Law Review* 86, No. 6 (2002), p. 1139.

9 "Rallying Americans to Defend Their Rights in a Digital Age: A Position Paper on Information Privacy," Privacy Revolution Web site, March 2009, p. 1. http://www.privacyrevolution.org/images/uploads/ALA_privacy_position_paper_MAR09_2.pdf.

Counterpoint: Laws and Courts Safeguard Privacy

1 California Constitution, Article I, §1.

2 *Overview of the Privacy Act of 1974, 2010 Edition*, U.S. Department of Justice Web site, December 2010. http://www.justice.gov/opcl/1974privacyact-overview.htm.

3 Samuel Warren and Louis D. Brandeis, "The Right to Privacy," *Harvard Law Review* 4, No. 5 (December 15, 1890), pp. 198–200.

4 *Griswold v. Connecticut*, 381 U.S. 479, 482–483 (1965).

5 Ibid., p. 484.

NOTES ////▷

Point: Protection of State Secrets Requires Strict Restrictions on FOI

1 John Podesta, "Remarks on Government Secrecy vs. Disclosure," First Amendment Center, March 27, 1999. http://www.firstamendmentcenter.org/news.aspx?id=5631.

2 *Report of the Commission on Protecting and Reducing Government Secrecy*, Senate Document 105–2, 1997, p. XXI.

3 Ibid., p. XXII.

4 *ACLU v. FBI*, 429 F. Supp. 2d 179 (D.D.C. 2006).

5 Ibid.

6 Ibid.

7 *Azmy v. U.S. Department of Defense*, 562 F.Supp. 2d 590 (S.D.N.Y., 2008).

8 32 CFR § 701.31.

9 *CIA v. Sims*, 471 U.S. 159, 178 (1985).

10 Ted Gup, *Nation of Secrets* (New York: Doubleday, 2007), p. 17.

11 148 *Congressional Record* H5647 (daily ed. July 25, 2002).

Counterpoint: Democracy Requires Inspection of State Secrets

1 Ronald Goldfarb, *In Confidence* (Ann Arbor, Mich.: Sheridan Books, 2009), p. 38.

2 Dan Froomkin, "Was Lack of Government Transparency a Factor in Mine Deaths?" *Huffington Post*, April 14, 2010. http://www.huffingtonpost.com/2010/04/14/was-lack-of-government-tr_n_537281.html.

3 Ibid.

4 Michael Moss, "Pentagon Study Links Fatalities to Body Armor," *New York Times*, January 7, 2006.

5 Information Security Oversight Office, *Report to the President 2009*, March 2010. http://www.archives.gov/isoo/reports/2009-annual-report.pdf.

6 Information Security Oversight Office, *Report to the President 2007*, May 2008. http://www.archives.gov/isoo/reports/2007-annual-report.pdf.

7 "Too Many Secrets: Overclassification as a Barrier to Critical Information Sharing," *Hearings Before the Subcommittee on National Security, Emerging Threats and International Relations of the Committee on Government Reform*, August 24, 2004 (Washington, D.C.: U.S. Government Printing Office, 2005), p. 1.

8 Scott Shane, "Since 2001, Sharp Increase in the Number of Documents Classified by the Government," *New York Times*, July 3, 2005.

9 "Drowning in a Sea of Faux Secrets: Policies on Handling of Classified and Sensitive Information," *Hearings Before the Subcommittee on National Security, Emerging Threats and International Relations of the Committee on Government Reform*, March 14, 2006 (Washington, D.C.: U.S. Government Printing Office, 2006), p. 2.

10 Steven Aftergood, "Reducing Government Secrecy: Finding What Works," *Yale Law & Policy Review* 27, No. 2 (Spring 2009), p. 415.

11 Minority Staff of Senate Committee on Government Reform, *Secrecy in the Bush Administration*, 108th Cong. 2nd sess., 2004. http://www.fas.org/sgp/library/waxman.pdf.

12 J. William Leonard, "A New Balancing Test: How Excessive Classification Undermines National Security," First Amendment Center Web site, March 14, 2008. http://www.firstamendmentcenter.org/about.aspx?id=19796.

13 "Drowning in a Sea of Faux Secrets," p. 5.

14 Ibid., p. 1.

15 "Emerging Threats: Overclassification and Pseudo-classification," *Hearings Before the Subcommittee on National Security, Emerging Threats and International Relations of the Committee on Government Reform*, March 2, 2005 (Washington, D.C.: U.S. Government Printing Office, 2005), p. 88.

16 "Joint Inquiry into Intelligence Community Activities Before and After the Terrorist Attacks of September 11, 2001," *Report of the U.S. Senate Select Committee on Intelligence and U.S. House Permanent Select Committee on Intelligence,* December 2002, pp. 123–124. http://www.gpoaccess.gov/serialset/creports/pdf/fullreport_errata.pdf.

17 Martin E. Halstuk and Eric B. Easton, "Of Secrets and Spies: Strengthening the Public's Right to Know about the CIA,"

Stanford Law & Policy Review 17, No. 2 (2006), p. 355.

18 Statement of Judy Loether, transcript of Panel Discussion of State Secrets, Constitution Project at the National Press Club, The Constitution Project Web site, January 24, 2008, p. 7. http://www.constitutionproject.org/manage/file/329.pdf.

19 Petition of Patricia J. Herring, et al., for a Writ of Error *Coram Nobis* to Remedy Fraud upon This Court, Federation of American Scientists Web site, February 26, 2003, p.1. http://www.fas.org/sgp/othergov/reynoldspet.pdf.

20 Aftergood, "Reducing Government Secrecy," p. 403.

21 U.S. Atomic Energy Commission memo, April 17, 1947. http://www.fas.org/sgp/othergov/doe/aec1947.pdf.

22 Aftergood, "Reducing Government Secrecy," pp. 403–404.

23 Goldfarb, *In Confidence*, p. 38.

Point: Targeted Transparency Effectively Promotes Freedom of Information

1 Archon Fung and Dara O'Rourke, "Reinventing Environmental Regulation from the Grassroots Up: Explaining and Expanding the Success of the Toxics Release Inventory," *Environmental Management* 25, No. 2 (February 2000), p. 118.

2 U.S. Environmental Protection Agency Web site, *U.S. EPA Toxics Release Inventory—2006 Public Data Release: Key Findings*, February 21, 2008. http://www.epa.gov/tri/tridata/tri06/pdr/key_findings_v12a.pdf.

3 Keith Bradsher, "Congress Appears Ready to Tackle Vehicle Rollover Problem," *New York Times*, September 21, 2000.

4 Testimony of Jeffrey W. Runge, M.D., administrator of the National Highway Traffic Safety Administration, Before the U.S. House Subcommittee on Commerce, Trade, and Consumer Protection, February 28, 2002. http://www.nhtsa.gov/nhtsa/announce/testimony/tread.html.

5 *Vehicle Safety: Opportunities Exist to Enhance NHTSA's New Car Assessment Program*, U.S. Government Accountability Office Web site, April 2005, p. 38. http://www.gao.gov/cgi-bin/getrpt?GAO-05-370.

6 U.S. Centers for Disease Control and Prevention Web site, *Food Safety*, July 31, 2009. http://www.cdc.gov/foodsafety.

7 Timothy F. Jones and Frederick J. Angulo, "Eating in Restaurants: A Risk Factor for Foodborne Disease?" *Clinical Infectious Diseases* 43, No. 10 (November 15, 2006), p. 1324.

8 Glenn Collins, "City Restaurants Required to Post Cleanliness Grades," *New York Times*, March 16, 2010.

9 Archon Fung, Mary Graham, and David Weil, *Full Disclosure: The Perils and Promise of Transparency* (New York: Cambridge University Press, 2007), p. 6.

Counterpoint: Targeted Transparency Laws Are Flawed

1 American Presidency Project, "Statement on Signing the Transportation Recall Enhancement, Accountability, and Documentation (TREAD) Act," November 1, 2000. http://www.presidency.ucsb.edu/ws/?pid=1085.

2 Neil J. Hoxie, Jeffrey P. Davis, James M. Vergeront, Raymond D. Nashold, and Kathleen A. Blair, "Cryptosporidiosis-Associated Mortality Following a Massive Waterborne Outbreak in Milwaukee, Wisconsin," *American Journal of Public Health* 87, No. 12 (December 1997), p. 2032.

3 *Safe Drinking Water Act Amendments of 1995*, Public Law 104-182, 104th Cong., 1st sess. (November 29, 1995).

4 Center for Science in the Public Interest Web site, "CSPI Urges FDA Crackdown on False & Misleading Food Labeling," December 29, 2009. http://www.cspinet.org/new/200912291.html.

5 Elena Fagotto and Archon Fung, "Improving Workplace Hazard Communication," *Issues in Science and Technology* (Winter 2002), p. 65.

6 Philip Zimbardo and Bruce Kluger, "Overcoming Terror," *Psychology*

Today Web site, July 1, 2003.
http://www.psychologytoday.com/
node/24822.

7 Ibid.

8 Linda T. Kohn, Janet M. Corrigan, and
Molla S. Donaldson, eds., *To Err Is
Human: Building a Safer Health System*
(Washington, D.C.: National Academies
Press, 2000), p. 1.

9 Kevin Jewell and Lisa McGiffert, "To Err
Is Human—To Delay Is Deadly," Safe
Patient Project Web site, May 2009, p.
2. http://www.safepatientproject.org/
pdf/safepatientproject.org-to_delay_is_
deadly-2009_05.pdf.

10 David Weil, "Targeted Transparency:
Transparency Policies Only Work If
They Give Users the Information They
Need, When They Need It, and in
the Form They Need For Making an
Effective Decision," *Public Manager*
38, No. 1 (Spring 2009), pp. 22–25.
http://www.thefreelibrary.com/Tar-
geted transparency: transparency
policies only work if they give. . .-
a0199538268.

Conclusion: A Matter of Balance

1 123 *Stat.* 2184 (2009).

2 James T. O'Reilly, *Federal Information
Disclosure, Vol. 2*, 3rd Ed. (Eagan, Minn.:
West Group, 2000, 2009), p. 86.

3 Craig D. Feiser, "Privatization and the
Freedom of Information Act: An Analysis of Public Access to Private Entities
Under Federal Law," *Federal Communications Law Journal* 52, No. 1 (December 1999), p. 22.

4 Beth Givens, "Public Records on the
Internet: The Privacy Dilemma," Privacy
Rights Clearinghouse Web site, revised
March 2006. http://www.privacyrights.
org/ar/onlinepubrecs.htm.

5 John Podesta, "Remarks on Government
Secrecy vs. Disclosure," First Amendment Center Web site, March 27, 1999.
http://www.firstamendmentcenter.org/
news.aspx?id=5631.

6 Vivek Kundra, "Data.gov: Pretty
Advanced for a One-Year-Old," White
House Web site, May 21, 2010. http://
www.whitehouse.gov/blog/2010/05/21/
datagov-pretty-advanced-a-one-year-old.

Books, Articles, and Reports

Aftergood, Steven. "Reducing Government Secrecy: Finding What Works." *Yale Law & Policy Review* 27, No. 2 (Spring 2009).

Banisar, David. *Freedom of Information Around the World 2006.* Privacy International Web site, 2006. Available online. URL: http://www. privacyinternational.org/foi/foisurvey2006.pdf.

Cassady, Alison, and Alex Fidis. "Toxic Pollution and Health." Washington, D.C.: U.S. PIRG Education Fund, 2007.

Collins, Glenn. "City Restaurants Required to Post Cleanliness Grades." *New York Times*, March 16, 2010.

Conrad, James W. Jr. "Open Secrets: The Widespread Availability of Information About the Health and Environmental Effects of Chemicals." *Law and Contemporary Problems* 69, No. 3 (Summer 2006).

Foerstel, Herbert N. *Freedom of Information and the Right to Know: The Origins and Applications of the Freedom of Information Act.* Westport, Conn.: Greenwood Press, 1999.

Fung, Archon, and Dara O'Rourke. "Reinventing Environmental Regulation from the Grassroots Up: Explaining and Expanding the Success of the Toxics Release Inventory." *Environmental Management* 25, No. 2 (Winter 2000).

Fung, Archon, Mary Graham, and David Weil. *Full Disclosure: The Perils and Promise of Transparency.* New York: Cambridge University Press, 2007.

Gardner, Amanda. "With Faulty Food Labeling, Who's Minding the Store?" *HealthDay News*, March 19, 2010.

Ginsberg, Wendy R. "Access to Government Information in the United States," Congressional Research Service, 2009. Available online. URL: http://www.fas.org/sgp/crs/secrecy/97-71.pdf.

Goldfarb, Ronald. *In Confidence.* New Haven: Yale University Press, 2009.

Graham, Mary. *Democracy by Disclosure: The Rise of Technopopulism.* Washington, D.C.: Brookings Institute, 2002.

Gup, Ted. *Nation of Secrets.* New York: Doubleday, 2007.

Hammitt, Harry A., Marc Rotenberg, John A. Verdi, and Mark S. Zaid, eds. *Litigation Under the Federal Open Government Laws 2008*. Washington, D.C.: EPIC Publications, 2008.

Holusha, John. "The Nation's Polluters—Who Emits What, and Where." *New York Times*, October 13, 1991.

Klosek, Jacqueline. *The Right to Know*. Santa Barbara, Calif.: ABC-CLIO, 2009.

Lane, Frederick S. *American Privacy*. Boston: Beacon Press, 2009.

Lathrop, Daniel, and Laurel Ruma, eds. *Open Government*. Sebastopol, Calif.: O'Reilly Media, 2010.

Lichtblau, Eric. "Social Security Opened Its Files for 9/11 Inquiry." *New York Times*, June 22, 2005.

McCrann, Grace-Ellen. "An Examination of the Conditions Surrounding the Passage of the 1966 U.S. Freedom of Information Act." *Open Government: A Journal on Freedom of Information* 3 (April 2007).

McDermott, Patrice. *Who Needs to Know?* Lanham, Md.: Bernan Press, 2007.

Moss, Michael. "Pentagon Acts on Body Armor." *New York Times*, January 21, 2006.

O'Reilly, James T. *Federal Information Disclosure,* 3rd Ed. Eagan, Minn.: West Group, 2000, 2009.

Pozen, David E. "The Mosaic Theory, National Security, and the Freedom of Information Act." *Yale Law Journal* 115, No. 3 (December 2005).

Rasky, Susan F. "Congress and E.P.A. Work on Programs to Identify Hazards." *New York Times*, August 19, 1985.

Reese, Shawn. "Homeland Security Advisory System: Possible Issues for Congressional Oversight." Washington, D.C.: Congressional Research Service, 2003.

Rothstein, Mark A. "Keeping Your Genes Private." *Scientific American*, September 2008.

Savage, David G. "Government Says No Privacy for Employee Messages." *Los Angeles Times*, April 19, 2010.

Sengupta, Somini. "Decades Later, Toxic Sludge Torments Bhopal." *New York Times*, July 7, 2008.

Shane, Scott. "Since 2001, Sharp Increase in the Number of Documents Classified by the Government." *New York Times*, July 3, 2005.

Siegel, Barry. *Claim of Privilege*. New York: HarperCollins Publishers, 2008.

Silverglade, Bruce, and Ilene Ringel Heller. *Food Labeling Chaos: The Case for Reform*. Washington, D.C.: Center for Science in the Public Interest, 2010.

Simon, Paul A., Phillip Leslie, Grace Run, Ginger Zhe Jin, Roshan Reporter, Arturo Aguirre, and Jonathan E. Fielding. "Impact of Restaurant Hygiene Grade Cards on Foodborne-Disease Hospitalizations in Los Angeles County." *Journal of Environmental Health* 67, No. 7 (March 2005).

Smith, Robert Ellis. *Ben Franklin's Web Site*. Providence, R.I.: Privacy Journal, 2000.

Solove, Daniel J. "Access and Aggregation: Public Records, Privacy and the Constitution." *Minnesota Law Review* 86, No. 6 (2002).

Soma, John T., and Stephen D. Rynerson. *Privacy Law*. St. Paul, Minn.: Thomson/West, 2008.

Stolberg, Sheryl Gay. "Obama Finds That Washington's Habits of Secrecy Die Hard." *New York Times*, April 5, 2009.

Tyler, Patrick E. "War in the Gulf: Military Analysis; Gulf Outlook: No Quick Victory in Sight." *New York Times*, January 24, 1991.

Weil, David, Archon Fung, Mary Graham, and Elena Fagotto. "The Effectiveness of Regulatory Disclosure Policies." *Journal of Policy Analysis and Management* 25, No. 1 (Winter 2006).

Weisman, Steven R. "Bhopal Is in Midst of Grim Recovery a Year After Leak." *New York Times*, December 1, 1985.

Web Sites

American Civil Liberties Union

http://www.aclu.org
> The ACLU's National Security Project promotes civil liberties and human rights by litigating cases relating to discrimination, surveillance, censorship, detention, and torture.

Electronic Frontier Foundation

http://www.eff.org

The EFF promotes the development and use of technologies to hold government agencies and corporations accountable to the public. For example, the organization's FOIA Litigation for Accountable Government Project has the goal of exposing the invasion of American citizens' privacy by governmental use of technologies.

Electronic Privacy Information Center

http://epic.org

EPIC, a public-interest research center, promotes an open government through its court battles. The EPIC Web site offers information about its court cases and images of documents obtained by FOIA requests.

Heritage Foundation

http://www.heritage.org

This think tank aims to promote conservative public policies based on the principles of "free enterprise, limited government, individual freedom, traditional American values, and a strong national defense." The organization provides FOIA-related news and criticism about government activities regarding freedom of information.

National Freedom of Information Coalition

http://www.nfoic.org/index.cfm

The NFOIC's Web site offers news about current and past efforts to obtain information under open-records laws, as well as reports on various aspects of open-government programs.

Open Government Initiative

http://www.whitehouse.gov/open

President Obama's Open Government Initiative strives to create a more open and accountable government. The Open Government Initiative Web site provides information about government activities, including government agencies' efforts to meet the new standard of openness.

Reporters Committee for Freedom of the Press

http://www.rcfp.org/

The group offers insights about FOI court cases, guidelines for using FOI laws, and the online journal *News Media & The Law*.

Society of Professional Journalists

http://www.spj.org/index.asp

This organization provides a list of state-by-state freedom of information contacts and resources, and news about FOI efforts.

Sunshine in Government Initiative

http://www.sunshineingovernment.org/

This coalition of media groups provides information on FOI issues and news stories about FOI law successes and failures.

PAGE

19: Staff/MCT/Newscom
29: Photo/goe/stf/ld/AP Images
47: AP Images

55: AP Images
66: Newscom

PHILL JONES earned a Ph.D. in physiology/pharmacology from the University of California, San Diego. After completing postdoctoral training at Stanford University School of Medicine, he joined the Department of Biochemistry at the University of Kentucky Medical Center as an assistant professor. He later earned a J.D. at the University of Kentucky College of Law and worked 10 years as a patent attorney, specializing in biological, chemical, and medical inventions. Phill Jones is now a full-time writer. His articles on various topics of law have appeared in *Biotechnology Law Report, Journal of the Patent and Trademark Office Society, Genetic Engineering News, Information Systems for Biotechnology News Report, Journal of BioLaw & Business, Food and Drug Law Journal, Modern Drug Discovery, Nature Biotechnology, Law and Order Magazine, History Magazine, PharmaTechnology Magazine,* and *Regulatory Affairs Focus.*

ALAN MARZILLI, M.A., J.D., lives in Washington, D.C., and is a senior writer for Advocates for Human Potential, Inc., a research and consulting firm based in Sudbury, Mass., and Albany, N.Y. He primarily works on developing training and educational materials for agencies of the federal government on topics such as housing, mental health policy, employment, and transportation. He has spoken on mental health issues in 30 states, the District of Columbia, and Puerto Rico; his work has included training mental health administrators, nonprofit management and staff, and people with mental illnesses and their families on a wide variety of topics, including effective advocacy, community-based mental health services, and housing. He has written several handbooks and training curricula that are used nationally and as far away as the territory of Guam. He managed statewide and national mental health advocacy programs and worked for several public interest lobbying organizations while studying law at Georgetown University. He has written more than a dozen books, including numerous titles in the Point/Counterpoint series.